Y

YOU'RE ONLY YOUNG TWICE

by Ron Aldridge

JOSEF WEINBERGER PLAYS

LONDON

YOU'RE ONLY YOUNG TWICE
First published in 2002
by Josef Weinberger Ltd
12-14 Mortimer Street, London, W1T 3JJ
www.josef-weinberger.com
general.info@jwmail.co.uk

Reprinted 2005

ISBN 0 85676 259 8

Printed by Wrightson's, 2 & 3 Mallard Close, Earls Barton, Northants NN6 0JF.

YOU'RE ONLY YOUNG TWICE was first presented by Eastbourne Theatres in association with Paul Farrah on August 21st 2001 at the Devonshire Park Theatre, Eastbourne. The cast was as follows:

SUE	Linda Regan
RICHARD	Tony Verner
GORDON 'BROOKSIE' BROOKS	Brian Murphy
TOM	Victor Spinetti
JULIA	Carmen Silvera
ROSE	Judy Cornwell
GRACE	Margaret Ashcroft

Directed by Ron Aldridge
Designed by Julie Godfrey
Lighting designed by Gavin Davis
Associate Producer Ian Fricker

CAST OF CHARACTERS

(In order of appearance)

Sue

Richard

Gordon 'Brooksie' Brooks

Tom

Julia

Rose

Grace

The action takes place in the Lounge/Dining Room of Sue and Richard's house.

The time is the present.

ACT ONE

Scene One

The setting is the lounge/dining room of RICHARD *and* SUE'S *semi-detached Victorian house.*

Upstage right is the front door and a small hallway, opposite which are stairs leading off stage left. On the upstage wall of the hallway is a door leading to another room.

Entrance to the main room is through a large alcove, and along part of the back wall of the main room is a drinks cabinet, upon which there is a telephone. Upstage left of the main room is a door leading off to the kitchen.

The main playing area is divided; stage right the lounge area, with sofa and armchair. Stage left the dining area, with a table and four chairs.

On the downstage left wall is a desk, on which are various ornaments, etc, including a framed photograph of GRACE, *and a table-lamp.*

On the stage right wall is a large bay window.

The feel is of a very comfortable 'lived-in' room. The style is very tasteful, and is a successful blend of both modern and antique.

It is late evening.

SUE *enters from the kitchen, crosses, and looks out of the window. She seems worried.*

RICHARD *enters from the kitchen, goes to the table and collects the two empty mugs. He stops and looks across at* SUE.

RICHARD Any sign of him yet?

SUE No.

RICHARD I told you. (*As he leaves.*) This is just ridiculous. Well, I'm not having it.

(*He exits into the kitchen.* SUE *crosses back and sits at the dining-table.* RICHARD *turns off the kitchen light as he enters.*)

RICHARD I'm going up. You coming?

SUE In a minute.

RICHARD You can't wait up all night for him, you know.

SUE I'm not going to wait up all night.

RICHARD It doesn't help.

SUE You go on. I won't be long. (*She suddenly stops.*) What was that?

RICHARD What? (*She hurries to the window and looks out.*) Oh this is ridiculous.

SUE I thought I heard him.

(*She turns and heads back to the table.*)

RICHARD Look at you. You've been jumping up and down like that for the last hour and a half. Well, I'm sorry, but it's just not on. It's not fair. He has no consideration for others whatsoever. I'm telling you, he won't be back yet. You know what he's like these days. Do you know what time he got in last night? Twenty past two. Twenty past two!

SUE I never heard him.

RICHARD You must be the only person in the street who didn't. It was disgraceful. Motorbike revving, car-doors slamming, car radio blaring, giggling, ages out there saying good night . . . no wonder he can't get up in the mornings.

SUE We don't want to stop him having a good time.

RICHARD And what about last Friday? Staying out all night.

SUE He did phone.

RICHARD Yeah, at a quarter to three in the morning. I blame that 'gang' he's got in with.

SUE Richard, please don't start that again. They're hardly tearaways.

RICHARD No, you're right, they're not tearaways. Terrorists, yes. I've never liked the look of any of them. Not one I'd trust. Drinking, dancing . . . you'd think there was nothing in life but pleasure.

SUE Don't exaggerate.

(*She gets up and crosses to the window again.*)

RICHARD I'm not exaggerating, and you know it. You let him get away with murder.

SUE It's just a harmless 'phase'. It'll pass.

RICHARD Harmless? You call being drunk and disorderly harmless?

SUE He's apologised for that.

RICHARD I knew it would happen. As soon as he got in with that 'gang', I knew it. He's got no discipline in his life. When was the last time he did any washing-up around here?

SUE Oh Richard, please.

RICHARD And have you seen the state of his room lately? He could grow mushrooms in there. He races in and out, treats this place like a hotel. And when he is here, he spends all his time on the telephone. He's just spent all day with them. What the hell else can there be to talk about? Well, I've had enough. I seriously think it's about time he found a place of his own.

Sue No Richard, not yet. He's not ready for that.

Richard It's got to happen sooner or later. And frankly, I'd rather it was sooner.

(*They hear a motorbike arrive.* Sue *hurries to the window.*)

Sue There he is! Oh, thank God he's safe.

Richard Safe? I'll give him safe.

Sue You know I don't like that motorbike.

Richard What are you talking about? You were the one who agreed to it in the first place.

Sue All right, all right. I just didn't want to –

Richard I was the one who said no. And a fat lot of good that did.

Sue Now please, Richard, let's not have a huge scene when he comes in. I'm sick and tired of you two rowing all the time.

Richard Tell *him*, not me.

Sue You're as bad as each other. Try and be a little gentle with him.

Richard What, strangle him slowly you mean?

(Gordon 'Brooksie' Brooks *enters. He is wearing motor-cycle gear, and crash helmet. He is dancing and humming as he closes the front door and enters into the main room. He finds himself between* Richard *and* Sue, *and suddenly stops when he sees them. He looks from one to the other, and then takes his crash helmet off.*)

Brooksie Oh, hello. Still up?

Richard We were waiting for you.

BROOKSIE That's very kind of you.

RICHARD We're not being kind. Sue was very worried.

BROOKSIE Why, what happened?

RICHARD You idiot. You happened.

SUE Dad, you know I worry when you're out on that motorbike.

BROOKSIE I've told you not to worry. I've only had seven pints, and I kept below ninety all the way home.

(BROOKSIE *crosses to the table, drapes his jacket on the back of one of the chairs, and puts his helmet, gauntlets and scarf onto the table.*)

RICHARD That's not funny. And by the way, we were a little noisy last night, weren't we?

BROOKSIE Were you? I didn't hear anything.

RICHARD Not me, you.

BROOKSIE You said we.

RICHARD You know what I mean. And what about the neighbours?

BROOKSIE Were they being noisy, too?

RICHARD Right, that's it. Go to your room.

BROOKSIE What?

RICHARD You heard me. Go to your room.

SUE Richard.

BROOKSIE I'm not going to my room. I've got my friends coming round.

SUE Coming round? What . . . now?

RICHARD Those hooligans? I'm sorry, but if you think . . .

BROOKSIE They're on their way now. It's just that I travel faster on the bike. (SUE *reacts.*) Oh, sorry Sue.

RICHARD What do you think this place is? Social Centre for the local Darby and Joan club?

BROOKSIE You don't get Darby and Joan any more.

RICHARD Don't you get picky with me.

BROOKSIE It's Barbie and Ken these days, isn't it?

RICHARD Well, I'm sorry, but if you want to have . . .

SUE Richard, please . . .

RICHARD If you want late-night parties, then I suggest you find your own place.

BROOKSIE I will find my own place.

RICHARD }
BROOKSIE } And the sooner the better!

SUE Stop it, the pair of you. You're like a couple of kids.

BROOKSIE He started it.

RICHARD You started it.

SUE That's enough!

BROOKSIE Yes Richard, that's enough. Now go to your room!

RICHARD What did you say?

SUE Richard! (*She grabs* RICHARD *and ushers him towards the stairs.*) We'll talk about this in the morning. Now go on, I'll be up in a minute.

RICHARD Oh yes, take his side. Never stick up for me do you? (*He gets to the bottom of the stairs, turns, and points at* BROOKSIE.) And if I hear any noise you've had it!

(*He storms off up the stairs.*)

BROOKSIE Ooooh, I'm really scared.

SUE Dad please, I wish you wouldn't wind him up so.

BROOKSIE I told you what he'd be like before you married him. You were warned.

SUE Now stop that. The truth of the matter is, it's you that's being unreasonable, not him. It's his house too, not just mine.

BROOKSIE Well, you needn't worry, I'll be finding my own place soon.

SUE I don't want you to find your own place. I want you here. Mum would have wanted that, too. She wouldn't have wanted you living on your own in the state you were in.

BROOKSIE I'm quite capable of looking after myself, you know.

SUE You didn't even know how to work the washing machine. (*She looks at him a moment.*) Also, it's good for me to have you here. It helps me. But you're going too far, I mean, what would Mum say about all your goings-on?

BROOKSIE What? You think she'd want me to stay miserable? I've done miserable, and believe me, it's not very nice.

(*He moves to the desk, and picks up the photo of* GRACE.)

SUE I know that. Look Dad, it's great to see you so happy again, but you've gone to the extreme.

BROOKSIE (*to photo*) You hear this Grace? They think I'm being extreme.

SUE — I just want you to realise that other people live in this house, too.

(*They hear a car arriving. The horn beeps loudly.*)

BROOKSIE — You want me to send them away?

SUE — Oh, Dad . . .

BROOKSIE — I will if you want.

SUE — No. No, it's all right.

BROOKSIE — Thanks, Sue. (*He excitedly hands* SUE *the photo, and heads for the front door.*) It's just that we're celebrating Tom and Julia's wedding.

SUE — The wedding? You've been celebrating that for a week already and they don't get married till Saturday.

BROOKSIE — They're making the most of their last few nights of freedom.

(*He gets to the front door.*)

SUE — And please tell them to be quiet. This is not easy for Richard,

(*He hurries out to greet them.*)

SUE — (*to photo*) I didn't realise he was this much trouble, Mum.

(*She repositions the photo on the desk.* BROOKSIE *and the 'gang'* – TOM, JULIA, *and* ROSE, *all in their 60s – enter very noisily.*)

SUE — Ssssh. Ssssh!

JULIA — Hello Sue. Sorry, I hope we're not too late.

SUE No no, it's fine. Hello Tom.

TOM Don't worry Sue, I'll keep them in order.

SUE Oh that's really put my mind at rest.

JULIA Sue, I don't think you've met my friend Rose.

SUE No, I haven't. Nice to meet you, Rose.

(ROSE *moves across to shake* SUE's *hand.*)

ROSE If this is at all inconvenient we'd be quite happy to leave.

SUE No no, it's all right Rose, honestly.

ROSE We know what Brooksie's like.

SUE It's fine. I'm off to bed now anyway. Good night all.

(*She heads for the stairs. They all say their good nights, a little too noisily. She hastily quietens them.*)

And please . . . try to keep the noise down. (*She turns to* BROOKSIE.) And not too late.

(*She heads off up the stairs.*)

BROOKSIE Right. Who's for some wine?

TOM Yeah, come on Brooksie, get the splosh out. We need something to help us recover from that film.

(BROOKSIE *heads to the drinks cabinet, and pours the drinks.*)

JULIA (*to* TOM, *as she sits on the sofa*) Well I don't care what you say, I thought it was a lovely film.

ROSE So did I.

Tom — Lovely film? It was total nonsense. That's the trouble with the world today, no decent films.

(Brooksie *hands a drink to* Rose.)

Brooksie — There you go, Rose. That should keep your nylons up.

(Rose *just looks at him, and then sits beside* Julia *on the sofa.* Brooksie *then continues to egg* Tom *on.*)

No, Tom's right. They don't make films like they used to.

Tom — No. Not like in our day.

Brooksie — (*still egging him on*) We had proper films then, with proper film stars.

Tom — That's right. There's no proper film stars these days. It's all different now. And I'll tell you when it changed. The rot all started with that Marlon Brando.

Julia — Marlon Brando? (Brooksie *gives a drink to* Julia.) Thanks.

Tom — You go and watch a film nowadays and everybody's mumbling. Can't understand a word they're saying. He started all that, Marlon Brando.

Rose — It's called method acting.

Tom — Huh. Some bloody method that is, when you don't know what's going on.

Brooksie — (*still egging him on*) He wasn't a proper film star, you see.

Tom — That's right. Not like old whatsisname. You know, the one with the moustache and the big ears.

JULIA Moustache and big ears?

TOM You know, the one in *Gone With The Wind*.

BROOKSIE Vivien Leigh.

TOM Idiot.

ROSE Clark Gable.

TOM Clark Gable. Now that's what you call a film star. Didn't matter that he had big ears, he could talk properly.

BROOKSIE (*handing a drink to* TOM) No mumbling when he was on.

TOM That's right. You always knew where you stood with him. He always played the hero. Bette Davis, she was always the villainess. Ava Gardner, she was always the beauty.

BROOKSIE Charlie Chan.

TOM Charlie Chan . . . Charlie Chan?

BROOKSIE He always took the Chinese parts.

TOM Yeah, he always took . . . excuse me, I'm being serious here.

BROOKSIE Sorry.

TOM Trouble is, it's all sex and violence these days. People don't want to see that in a film. You get enough of that on the streets.

BROOKSIE (*hurries to look out of the window*) Do you?

TOM Brooksie!

BROOKSIE Sorry.

TOM And where have all those wonderful musicals gone? Haven't had a decent one of those since *The Sound of Music*. Millions flocked in to see it. Innocent, you see. That's the trouble with the world today, not enough innocence. Kids grow up too quickly. Six-year-olds look like sixteen-year-olds. Wandering around in frocks and make-up.

BROOKSIE — And that's just the boys.

TOM — Yeah, that's just the . . .

BROOKSIE — Sorry.

TOM — Oh, what's the point of talking to you lot! You don't care. The world is falling apart, and you don't care.

JULIA — Oh, don't be so dramatic.

TOM — You don't think the world is falling apart? My poor old mum would turn in her grave if she could see some of the things happening nowadays. Do you know what I read in the local paper the other day? The police caught a murderer who was sitting on the top deck of a number 36 bus with a severed head in his suitcase. I mean, that's incredible isn't it?

JULIA — Certainly is. He was lucky to find a 36 bus.

ROSE — Stop being such a gloom and doom merchant, Tom. This is supposed to be a really happy time for you. You're getting married in two days' time.

BROOKSIE — Yeah, chirpen up.

TOM — Chirpen up? What sort of language is that?

JULIA — Two days. I can't believe it's really going to happen.

BROOKSIE — It's going to happen Julia. And I think we should toast to it. A proper toast!

JULIA — Oh no.

BROOKSIE — Oh yes. Now come on.

(*He gets* JULIA *up*.)

TOM We don't need another toast.

BROOKSIE Of course we do. Come on, up you get.

(*He gets* TOM *up*.)

ROSE Please, can't we just do an ordinary toast?

BROOKSIE Definitely not. Now come on. It's not every week we have a wedding to celebrate.

(*He gets* ROSE *up*.)

ROSE This is stupid.

BROOKSIE This is fun, Rose. Know what fun means? Here we go then, gang. In position. But quietly! One, two, three, four . . .

(*They go into their choreographed routine while chanting the following rap-style chorus: they start in a circle, jigging on the spot*.)

"Here's to the wedding of Tom and Julia,
Some might think that the union is peculiar,
But we don't think so, we think it's great,
So here's to the wedding, and don't be late!"

BROOKSIE One, two, three, four . . .

(*They sing the chorus again, but this time the dancing becomes more lively. The ladies change places across the circle, jive-style, during the first two lines, then the men change places during the last two lines*.)

BROOKSIE One, two, three, four . . .

(*This time, even more lively, they sing the tune of 'In the Mood' as they make a large circle, collecting their glasses from the table as they pass, ending with their glasses raised together for the final toast as they sing just the last line.*)

So here's to the wedding and don't be late.
Yeah!

(*They end up slightly breathless and laughing, all except* Rose, *who is clearly not enjoying herself.*)

Brooksie — Oh, well done. That was great, eh Rose?

Rose — It was not great at all but at least it wasn't as embarrassing as doing it in the middle of the Over-60s club.

Tom — Now that was great. We nearly got thrown out after the third time. I've never nearly been thrown out of anywhere before.

(Brooksie *offers* Julia *some more wine*.)

Julia — No more please Brooksie, I'm not used to all this drinking.

Brooksie — Yes, I suppose you ought to be a bit careful. Don't want him taking advantage of you before the wedding night.

Julia — Ooh no, I want to save myself.

Tom — (*spluttering*) From what?

Brooksie — Rose is saving herself for our first date, right Rose?

Rose — A date with you? I'd rather crawl over broken glass.

Julia — (*sitting on the sofa*) Well, let's hope it doesn't come to that.

Rose — You've got more chance of a date with Joan Collins.

Brooksie Joan Co . . . what, the woman at number 55?

Rose No, idiot, not the woman at . . . Joan Collins the film star.

Brooksie Oh, her. No, she's not my type. But the woman at number 55 . . .

Julia Oh Rose, you know Sally Beaumont? She says that for the wedding she's getting her hair done like Joan Collins.

Rose Really?

Brooksie That should be interesting. Hair like Joan Collins and a figure like Sylvester Stallone.

Julia Brooksie!

Rose Don't be so horrible.

Brooksie What? I'm only telling the truth. Come on, be honest, that is a woman who would not look out of place in a ring with Frank Bruno.

Julia Don't be so mean. She's very nice.

Rose He's not interested in nice, Julia. It's the tarty ones he goes after.

Tom Yeah, like that woman at number 55.

Rose (*to* Brooksie) You're a bad influence, and I don't like it.

Brooksie Bad influence? What's brought this on?

Rose Everything's a joke with you, isn't it? Life isn't all about fun and laughter you know.

Brooksie It isn't all about being serious either, Rose.

Tom Yes, be fair Rose. Life has got much better for all of us since Brooksie arrived.

Rose Not for all of us.

TOM — It's livelier, more fun . . . and he's helped people, you know he has.

ROSE — That doesn't excuse the other things he's done.

TOM — I've seen him Rose. He stops people worrying about their aches and pains all the time.

ROSE — The reason they stop worrying about their aches and pains is because they're more worried about what he's doing with his hands. He flirts with all the widows at the Over-60s club, and tries to tinker with quite a few of them, too.

BROOKSIE — I do not tinker.

ROSE — What about poor Elaine then?

BROOKSIE — Oh come on. It was just a bit of fun.

ROSE — See what I mean? Fun again.

BROOKSIE — She got too serious. She was all for settling down. I don't want that. (*He turns to* ROSE.) And I don't know what it is you think happens . . . because nothing actually happens, you know. I'm not some rampaging ageing Don Juan. The truth is that if it wasn't for pickpockets and frisking at airports I wouldn't have any sex life at all. Anyway, I'm already married. (*He crosses to the desk and looks at the photo of* GRACE.) My Grace might not be with me any more, but as far as I'm concerned, she's still my wife.

ROSE — We've all lost our spouses, we know what you've been through. We've been hurt just as much as you have. But we also understand that life goes on. The only difference is, we don't deliberately take it out on other people.

BROOKSIE I'm not deliberately taking it out on other people.

ROSE You don't care, it's the same thing.

BROOKSIE I don't want to be pinned down, that's all. Unless it's by you of course, Rose. You can pin me down any time you like.

ROSE There you go again. Why do you have to be so vulgar?

BROOKSIE That's a very interesting question, Rose. Tell you what, once they've gone off on honeymoon, we'll go out on a date and discuss it.

ROSE The only thing I want to discuss with you are funeral arrangements.

(ROSE *heads across and sits on the sofa.*)

JULIA Oh come on you two, stop squabbling.

TOM Anyway, we might not ever get on honeymoon.

BROOKSIE What do you mean? I thought you'd already booked it.

TOM I tried. But she doesn't want to fly.

JULIA You know I hate flying.

TOM Safest form of transport, flying. Always has been, always will be.

JULIA It's all right for you. You were in the RAF, you're used to it,

BROOKSIE No no, Tom's right. Flying is safe. It's the crashing that's dangerous.

TOM You've got more chance of being run over by a bus.

JULIA — And I always seem to end up sitting at the back. It's horrible.

TOM — Ah, you want to sit up the front. In the cockpit, that's the best place.

BROOKSIE — Personally, I've always thought that the best place to sit was next to that black box.

(TOM *moves and sits in the armchair.*)

TOM — The point is this. It doesn't matter if you're crossing the road, driving a car, or flying in a plane. If your number's up, your number's up.

JULIA — I can accept that. What does concern me, though, is if I'm sitting on the plane when the pilot's number comes up.

ROSE — Well, the only thought I keep having as I hurtle through the skies is that every part of this machine was supplied by the lowest bidder.

JULIA — Anyway, I don't want to talk about it any more. We'll sort it out tomorrow.

TOM — What are we all doing tomorrow, by the way?

BROOKSIE — What are you talking about? We've got the stag night.

(BROOKSIE *pulls out and sits astride one of the chairs from the table.*)

TOM — I mean during the day.

JULIA — And we need to decide where we're going for our hen-night. Rose suggested we went to see some male strippers, but I'm not so sure.

ROSE — I did not.

BROOKSIE — Rose, you saucy little rascal.

ROSE — I suggested no such thing.

BROOKSIE Anyway, what do you want to see them for when you've got us, eh Tom?

(ROSE *and* JULIA *just look at each other.*)

TOM Oh I don't know. In my younger days people used to be very envious of my physique. Now they just look at me and sigh with relief.

JULIA So come on, what are we going to do?

TOM No more films please.

BROOKSIE Something gentle, as we've all got a long night ahead of us. How about meeting for lunch?

TOM We could go to Lorenzo's.

JULIA Oh no, let's not go there. I didn't like the ambience.

BROOKSIE You should have had the chicken. Tell you what, let's have lunch here.

JULIA Here? Are you sure?

BROOKSIE Richard and Sue are out all day. We'll have a game of something in the afternoon. How's that sound?

JULIA We'll bring the food.

TOM And as a special treat, I'll cook for us.

JULIA You? Cook the lunch?

TOM Yes. Me.

JULIA When was the last time you cooked a lunch? Must be the best part of forty years.

TOM I'll have you know I'm a very good cook. I learned when I was in the RAF.

BROOKSIE And how long ago is that? You were in the RAF before they had planes.

ROSE I'll cook the lunch.

BROOKSIE Oh no, sorry Rose, I've heard about your cooking. She's what you call a religious cook. Everything she serves up is either a sacrifice or a burnt offering.

ROSE (*suddenly getting up*) You stupid, stupid man!

BROOKSIE All right Rose, calm down, it was just a joke.

ROSE Everything's a joke isn't it? Well these others may think you're Mr Wonderful, but be assured, I most definitely do not.

(BROOKSIE *gets up and moves across to her.*)

BROOKSIE Excuse me, but have I done something to you? You've done nothing but snap at me all evening. What did you find out about me? That I'm a serial killer? That I murdered next door's kids?

TOM Actually that's not a bad idea. Do you know what those little bleeders did to my car?

JULIA Be quiet, Tom.

BROOKSIE Come on. What did I do?

ROSE You don't have to do anything. It's just you. You may be enjoying your second childhood, but frankly, some of us find it a bit pathetic.

BROOKSIE Pathetic, eh? Well let me tell you something. I don't give a tinker's cuss what you think. I've got one life. I've had enough of misery, enough of negativity, and enough of depression. Yes, I do intend to enjoy every day I've got left, and if you find that pathetic then that's your problem, not mine.

(*He angrily returns to sit on the chair. There is a silence.*)

TOM I think we'll start with a nice bowl of Rosie.

BROOKSIE What?

TOM Tomorrow's lunch. We'll start with a bowl of Rosie.

BROOKSIE What do you mean, bowl of Rosie?

TOM Rosie Loop, soup.

BROOKSIE Rosie Loop, soup? It's Rosie Lee, tea. Loop de Loop, soup.

TOM Loop de Loop, soup? Are you sure? Doesn't sound right to me.

ROSE Well if you'll all excuse me, I don't really feel like discussing tomorrow's menu. I'm very tired.

(*She puts her glass on the drinks cabinet, and moves towards the front door.*)

JULIA (*rising*) Yes, perhaps we ought to call it a night.

BROOKSIE But it's still early. We haven't got to the dancing yet.

JULIA We'll save it for tomorrow.

(*She puts her glass on the drinks cabinet.*)

TOM (*rising*) Yeah, save it for tomorrow, Brooksie.

BROOKSIE OK. (*He rises, puts the chair back at the table, and moves across to them.*) See you all tomorrow. Good night, Rose. Sleep well. Dream of me if you must, but no naughty dreams, OK?

ROSE Oh, please.

(*She leaves.*)

TOM — Take it easy on her, Brooksie.

JULIA — She is my best friend.

TOM — She's not used to enjoying herself. Good night.

BROOKSIE — Yeah, see you tomorrow. (*They leave.*) Mind how you trip over the step.

(*He closes the door behind them.*)

BROOKSIE — Not used to enjoying herself. So what is that? We all have to be miserable?

(*He turns off the main light. The light in the hallway is still on, and then he notices that the lamp on the desk is still on. He crosses to turn it off. The photo of* GRACE *is next to the lamp. As be is about to turn the lamp off, he sees the photo, stops, looks at it a moment, and then picks it up.*)

Oh Grace. We never liked being miserable, did we? "Never go to bed on a row", that's what you always said. No wonder we never got any sleep. Ah . . . my lovely Grace with the lovely face. I know you sometimes felt you had a face like a bag of spanners . . . but I never did. Remember how I used to wind you up with that song?

(*He starts to sing gently.*)

"I've grown accustomed to your face . . ."

(*He hums the next line as he looks at the photo.*)

And I used to love that dress, too.

(*He sings.*)

"That blue dress you used to wear . . ."

(*He hums the next line. He then sings.*)

"And that dance we used to do . . ."

(*He starts to dance, and then almost drops the photo.*)

BROOKSIE Oh! . . . Sorry, Grace.

(GRACE *'appears' from the shadows behind him, and slowly moves across to the light.*)

All this talk of weddings, Grace. Remember ours? Remember our honeymoon . . . how much we laughed? Two weeks of laughter.

(GRACE *moves into the pool of light.*)

GRACE I think your memory's a bit hazy, Brooksie. I seem to remember you being grumpy most of the time.

(*He continues to talk to the photo.*)

BROOKSIE I know I was a bit grumpy now and again.

GRACE Just because they didn't laugh at your speech.

BROOKSIE (*to photo*) It's because they didn't laugh at my speech. I think I should have rehearsed it a bit more.

GRACE It wouldn't have helped, believe me. It was just a stupid speech, why did you have to make it so important?

BROOKSIE (*to photo*) Why did I have to make it so important? I always worried too much about what people thought of me. And I'm still doing it, Grace, I'm still doing it. Oh Grace, I need you to talk to. It's not the same on my own. It's frightening. Sue says I've got too extreme. I wonder what you'd think?

GRACE I think you should stop tickling the widows so much.

Brooksie — (*to photo*) Maybe I should stop tickling the widows so much. But I don't mean any harm, Grace. And I have to tell you, some of them quite like it.

Grace — Don't try so hard Brooksie. You have wonderful qualities, don't hide them under this veneer of jollity. Relax. Be yourself.

Brooksie — The only person I could be myself with . . . (*He lowers the photo and looks at her.*) was you.

Grace — Well, that shows you can do it. And Rose was right. You were very naughty with Elaine.

Brooksie — I never touched her.

Grace — You know what I mean. And be gentle with Rose. She's a very lovely soul.

Brooksie — I try. She's the one that picks on me.

Grace — Be gentle with Richard and Sue as well. It is their house. And Sue is finding it hard without me.

Brooksie — So am I, Grace. So am I.

Grace — I know. That's why you must support each other. I want you to be happy, Brooksie, but don't make them unhappy. Find another way.

Brooksie — I know you're right, Grace, but it's difficult for me. I need you to help me. I'm just so . . . so lost without you. And I don't know where you are.

Grace — I'm with you, Brooksie, I'm still with you. And I'm all right. It's where I should be. I know you're lost, but we're going to change that. And it's time now.

Brooksie — Time? Time for what?

GRACE Time to change. Time for you to move forward. And when you look back, don't look back with sadness, look back with joyous rememberance at the time we had together. It wasn't cut short, whatever you may think, it was exactly the right time. And it was a wonderful time.

BROOKSIE It was.

GRACE But everything changes, Brooksie, and now we must change again. Up to now we've stayed 'connected'. But I have to move on, too.

BROOKSIE Move on? Where are you going?

GRACE I'll always be with you but you can't stay dependent. And I know you're still dependent on me, Brooksie, I hear your prayers at night. And you know, you really shouldn't swear when you're praying, it's not nice.

BROOKSIE Sorry.

GRACE Be gentle with yourself. People will still like you even if you don't tell jokes all the time.

BROOKSIE You'll have to help me, Grace.

GRACE I will. I'll always help you.

(*She places her hands on his head in a healing gesture.*)

And don't worry . . . I won't move on until you're ready.

(*Her hands come down, and she starts to move away from him.*)

So remember, Brooksie . . . no more bad jokes . . . (*She moves further away.*) . . . and try to let them see the real you.

BROOKSIE The real me.

(*She 'disappears' into the shadows.*)

Grace — Good night, Brooksie.

(Brooksie *looks back at the photo.*)

Brooksie — I've forgotten who the real me is.

(*He puts the photo back on the desk, turns out the lamp and crosses to the stairs. He gets to the stairs, stops, and turns back.*)

Good night, Grace.

(*He heads up the stairs. After a few moments, the hallway light snaps off.*)

End of Scene One.

Scene Two

It is the following afternoon.

The 'gang' – Brooksie, Tom, Julia, *and* Rose, *are sitting at the table playing* Trivial Pursuit.

Tom — Your go, Julia.

(Julia *throws the dice, and moves.*)

Julia — Oh no, Sport and Leisure.

Brooksie — (*taking a question card*) Who won the cup in 1968?

Julia — Oh, not football again. How do I know who won the cup? I don't even know what cup they're talking about.

Tom — Don't be so daft. The FA Cup. The FA Cup.

Julia — Don't call me daft.

Tom — Well, do you know or not?

JULIA Of course I don't know.

ROSE Give her another question.

TOM Hold on . . .

BROOKSIE I'll give her another question.

TOM . . . what are you doing? That's not in the rules.

BROOKSIE Calm down Tom, it's only a game.

TOM I'm sorry, but rules are rules.

BROOKSIE She doesn't know anything about football.

TOM What's that got to do with it? I don't know anything about sewing.

BROOKSIE All right, if you get a sewing question you can have another go, too.

(BROOKSIE *takes another question card.*)

TOM I'm sorry, but I'm not happy.

BROOKSIE Right, Julia. Who was the first Czechoslovakian to win the Wimbledon women's singles tennis title?

JULIA Oh, I know this. I know this . . . what'sername . . . you know . . . oh, it's on the tip of my tongue . . . don't tell me.

TOM Don't tell you? Of course we're not going to tell you. What sort of game do you think this is? Come on, do you know or not?

JULIA Will you stop being so crabby, I'm thinking.

TOM I think we should think about having a rule about thinking time, that's what I think.

BROOKSIE Will you shut up about rules. Julia?

JULIA Sorry, I can't remember.

Brooksie — Martina Navratilova.

Julia — I knew that. I knew that.

Tom — Tough. Your go, Brooksie.

(Brooksie *gets the dice.*)

Tom — And from now on, rules are rules, right?

Rose — God, it's pathetic. You men. It's not life and death, you know.

Tom — Come on, Brooksie, it's your go.

Brooksie — (*to* Rose) What do you mean, men? Don't include me.

Tom — Brooksie . . .

Brooksie — He's the one.

Rose — You're just as bad.

Brooksie — What have I done? Don't go picking on me for no reason.

Tom — Brooksie, throw the dice!

Brooksie — All right, all right, keep your tights on. (*He throws the dice, and moves.*) Art and Literature, please.

Tom — (*taking a question card*) Who wrote the Father Brown stories?

Brooksie — Chesterton.

(Brooksie *goes to get the dice to have another go.* Tom *stops him.*)

Tom — Hold it! That's not what I've got written here.

Brooksie — What are you talking about? It was Chesterton.

Tom — I'm sorry, but that's not what's written here.

Brooksie Who was it then?

Tom GK Chesterton.

Brooksie Well of course it's GK.

Tom Don't say of course. How do I know you meant GK? You could have been thinking about his brother Mick.

Brooksie His brother Mick? What the hell are you talking about?

Tom I'm sorry, but we must have the correct answer.

Julia He got it right Tom, come on.

Tom He didn't get it right.

Brooksie Oh don't be so ridiculous. It's my turn again.

(*He goes to get the dice.* Tom *quickly grabs it.*)

Tom Oh no you don't.

Brooksie Give me that dice.

Tom No.

Julia Oh come on, Tom.

Tom No, I said.

Brooksie If you don't give me that dice, I'm not playing.

Tom Don't play then.

Brooksie Right. I'm packing up the game.

Tom Oh, don't be so childish.

Brooksie It's my game.

Julia Give him the dice.

Tom No.

JULIA Give him the dice.

TOM No.

ROSE (*very loudly*) Give him the dice!

(TOM *almost jumps out of his seat. After a moment he reluctantly gives in.*)

TOM Oh, here, have it then!

(*He throws the dice to* BROOKSIE.)

BROOKSIE Thank you.

TOM Child.

(BROOKSIE *throws again, and moves.*)

BROOKSIE Entertainment, please.

TOM (*takes a question card*) Which actress has received the most Oscar nominations?

BROOKSIE Bette Davis.

TOM No! Katherine Hepburn. Hee hee. He got it wrong. He got it wrong. (*He is beside himself with glee. He starts to make childish 'na na na na na na' noises.*) Right. My go. (*He throws the dice, and moves.*)
Geography, please.

ROSE (*takes a question card*) What body of water borders Saudi Arabia to the East?

TOM The East? Oh that's easy. The Gulf. (*He goes for the dice again.*)

ROSE Hold it! That's not what's written here.

TOM What?

ROSE It's the Persian Gulf.

TOM I was talking about the Persian Gulf.

ROSE But you didn't say so. You might have been thinking about the Gulf of Mexico.

TOM But I wasn't.

JULIA Tough.

(*They all start making childish 'na na na na na na' noises back at him. He jumps up from the table.*)

TOM Right! That's it. I'm not playing any more.

JULIA Oh don't be such a baby. It was your idea to play the stupid game.

TOM Don't call me a baby.

JULIA I'd much rather have gone ten-pin bowling, wouldn't you Rose?

ROSE No.

TOM Bit of respect, please. That's the trouble with the world today, not enough respect.

JULIA No, the trouble with the world today is there are too many bad losers.

TOM I'm not a bad loser. I love losing.

BROOKSIE All right you two, all right. You carry on like this you'll be getting a divorce before you get married. Take it easy. Actually, a friend of mine's getting a divorce. Says his wife hasn't spoken to him for six months. I told him to think it over. Wives like that are hard to find.

ROSE Here we go again, more jokes.

BROOKSIE Don't start on me, Rose. (*He turns to* TOM.) Tell you what. I'll give you another question.

TOM I don't want another question.

Julia (*to* Brooksie) Oh go on, take his side.

Brooksie No, come on Julia, give him another chance.

Tom I'm not playing.

Brooksie Here, look, I'll give you a random question. If you get it right we carry on, if not we stop. (*He takes a card.*)

Tom I'm not interested.

Brooksie This is an Entertainment question. "If Ken Dodd's father's dog died, what would the headline be in the local paper?"

Tom What sort of question's that?

Brooksie I've told you. Entertainment.

Tom Let me see that.

(*He goes to grab the card.* Brooksie *pulls it away.*)

Brooksie Come on. "If Ken Dodd's father's dog died, what would the headline be in the local paper?"

Tom I'm not answering a stupid question like that.

Brooksie Answer. Ken Dodd's dad's dog's dead.

Tom You idiot. Well that's definitely it. Count me out.

(*He grabs two of the coffee cups and heads for the kitchen. He stops.*)

Stupid question. Ken Dodd's dids . . .

(*They all start laughing and making the childish noises at him again. He storms off into the kitchen.*)

Julia (*yelling after him*) Miserable little so-and-so!

Rose (*also yelling*) Yes, and I was winning, too!

Julia — I know. You're very good at this game, Rose. I'm hopeless. You'd think I'd be good at it with my memory. I've usually got a fantastic memory, it's amazing the things I remember. Did you know that in 1899 you could get six roasted larks in a tin for threepence ha'penny? It's true. I read it somewhere, and it stayed with me. I mean, why would the brain retain that sort of information? What good can it do me? Interesting that, isn't it?

Brooksie — Well . . .

Julia — And I'll tell you something else that's interesting too. I can remember all sorts of details about my life, dates and places and things, but do you know, for the life of me, I can't remember what I was doing on the day that John F Kennedy was assassinated. Isn't that extraordinary?

(*They all look at her for a moment.*)

Brooksie — Yes. Well, thank you for sharing that with the group, Julia. OK, who's go is it?

Rose — Mine.

Brooksie — (*yelling*) Tom!

(Tom *enters from the kitchen.*)

Tom — I've told you. I'm not playing any more.

Brooksie — That's all right. We can play without you.

(Tom *collects the other cups from the table, and again heads off into the kitchen.*)

Tom — Play without me then. Ken Dodd's dad's digs . . .

(*They again start the childish noises.*)

Brooksie — Come on then, we'll play without him.

Julia — (*rising*) No, I think we'd better call it a day, Brooksie.

Rose — Yes, you can have too much of a good thing.

Julia — We've still got a few things to arrange before tomorrow.

Rose — (*rising*) And I think I might go home for a little nap if we're in for a late night tonight.

Brooksie — You can have a little nap here if you want, Rose.

Julia — Brooksie, you naughty boy!

Rose — Take no notice, Julia. He gets these silly ideas. It's because he went for a brain transplant the other week, and the brain rejected him.

Brooksie — Rose! A joke. You made a joke.

(Tom *appears in the kitchen doorway. He is drying up one of the mugs*.)

Julia — Don't be horrible to Rose.

Brooksie — What do you mean, I've been very gentle with her today. I wouldn't be horrible, you know how I feel about Rose. Every time I see her the water on my knee bubbles. I still remember our first meeting. I took one look, and then I went all vague and misty-eyed.

Tom — I went like that once when my boxers got shrunk in the wash.

Julia — Come on you, stop messing about in that kitchen. We've got things to do.

Tom — I'm not messing about, I'm doing that lazy little tyke's dirty little work for him.

JULIA We need to get to the shops.

TOM Oh, yippee.

(*He exits into the kitchen.*)

JULIA I want to buy him some new clothes for the honeymoon.

BROOKSIE Oh yes, the honeymoon! Off to Paris through the Channel Tunnel.

JULIA I know. It's so exciting. I've never been to Paris before.

ROSE You'll love it.

JULIA Thought I'd better smarten him up a bit. Try and get him to look a little trendy.

(TOM *enters from the kitchen.*)

BROOKSIE Trendy? Him? You've got more chance of seeing the Pope at an orgy.

TOM I don't need any new clothes thank you very much.

JULIA Yes you do. I'm not having you traipsing up and down the Champs Elysées looking like a vagabond.

TOM Excuse me!

BROOKSIE Apparently, the latest fashion adorning the Paris streets at the moment, so I'm told, is pink frilly shirts.

JULIA Really?

BROOKSIE He'd look pretty in pink.

TOM And you'd look pretty in black and blue. Forget it. I'm happy as I am. What I'm not happy about is going through that tunnel.

Julia — There's nothing wrong with that tunnel. Anyway, it's better than flying.

Tom — It is not better than flying. I wouldn't mind if they had any decent trains. That's the trouble with the world today, no decent trains.

Brooksie — No, they don't make trains like they used to.

Tom — That's right. They should never have done away with steam trains. That's what you call a train.

Julia — Brooksie, will you stop winding him up.

Tom — Oh yes, I remember it like it was yesterday. Trundling down to Kings Cross with a weekend pass, snuggled up to a WAAF with the blinds down. What a life. Heady romantic days they were. That's the trouble with the world today, not enough romance.

Brooksie — Talking of romance, Rose . . .

Rose — Forget it. The answer's no.

Brooksie — I haven't asked anything yet.

Rose — It's still no.

Julia — Can we give you a lift anywhere, Rose?

Rose — No, it's all right thanks, Julia. I'll walk back.

Julia — Are you sure?

Rose — I'm quite sure. You carry on. I need to have a private word with Brooksie anyway.

Brooksie — You want a private word with me, Rose?

Rose — Yes, if that's all right.

Brooksie — Of course it's all right. (*He tries to hurriedly usher the others out.*) See you later then, Tom.

Tom — I'm not sure you should be left alone with him, Rose.

Rose — I'll be all right.

Julia — She'll be all right. Just make sure you two are all right tonight. No late-night drinking. You're not as young as you used to be.

Brooksie — Don't you worry about us, we're as fit as fiddles. In fact, if we were any healthier we'd be dangerous.

Julia — Yes. See you at eight, Rose.

Rose — Bye.

Tom — Bye, Rose. See you tomorrow.

(Brooksie *stops* Tom.)

Brooksie — Thanks for doing the lunch, Tom. What was it, by the way, in case I have to describe it to the doctor?

(*He closes the door and turns back to* Rose.)

A private word, eh? This is a bit of a surprise, Rose. I thought you were going home for a nap.

Rose — I am. But I'd like to get a few things sorted out between us first.

Brooksie — Oh. OK. Want a cup of tea?

Rose — No thank you.

Brooksie — You sure? It's no trouble.

Rose — (*firmly*) I said no thank you.

Brooksie — All right Rose, take it easy. It's only a cup of tea. I'm not asking you to dance naked on the table. Mind you, if you felt that way inclined, I'm not about to stop you. (*He stops as he sees her reaction.*) Sorry, Rose. Now, what did you want to talk about?

Rose — It's about tomorrow.

Brooksie — Tomorrow?

Rose — The wedding.

Brooksie — Oh yes, the wedding. What about it?

Rose — You are the best man and one of the witnesses. I am the other witness.

Brooksie — Yes.

Rose — We may need to do things together, and I do not want Julia's day spoilt.

Brooksie — Neither do I, Rose.

Rose — So I suggest we try to clear the air of our differences, implement a temporary reconciliation, and suspend hostilities at least until after the wedding.

Brooksie — Implement a reconciliation and suspend hostilities? That sounds a bit saucy, Rose.

Rose — Please, I'm being serious here.

Brooksie — Sorry. I was only trying . . .

Rose — Yes, I know what you're trying. Just don't, all right?

Brooksie — All right.

Rose — Do you agree?

Brooksie — Agree to what?

Rose — For goodness' sake. To what I've just said.

Brooksie — If it makes you happy, Rose, then yes, I agree.

ROSE I want no stupid jokes, no infantile behaviour, and no sarcastic jibes. Not with me. I don't care what you do with other people, but not with me. Is that clear?

BROOKSIE I'll try my best, Rose.

ROSE You'll try your best? I'm not sure that'll be good enough. I need more assurance than that.

BROOKSIE I cross my heart, I cross my legs, I cross everything humanly possible. I give you my word as a scholar and a gentleman, and I also offer you the ancient solemn oath of the Brooks's: 'Ipso fatso ibsy squibsy'. And if after that I should step out of line, Rose, I plead with the Almighty that a thunderbolt will shoot down and strike me . . .

ROSE Yes, all right, all right, you've made your point. God, it's like talking to a child. But I meant what I said, Brooksie. If you spoil tomorrow, I'll never forgive you. Right. I've said what I wanted to say. I'll see you at the Registry Office tomorrow.

(*She starts to leave.*)

BROOKSIE Don't go, Rose.

(*She stops.*)

ROSE I'm sorry, but I need a little nap.

(*She turns again to leave.*)

BROOKSIE No, hold on, Rose.

ROSE What?

BROOKSIE Look, I'm sorry. You've come here and said your piece, in all seriousness, and I've just been silly and flippant. I'm sorry, Rose, really. But please, there's a few things I'd like to say now, too. Please. Sit down.

ROSE Brooksie, I don't think . . .

BROOKSIE Please.

(*She reluctantly sits.*)

You just don't understand me, Rose, that's the problem.

ROSE I understand you perfectly well, thank you.

BROOKSIE I am but a mere mortal. A fly caught in the cobweb of life. I am a misunderstood person. It's because of my childhood, you see. I had a very bad start in life.

ROSE Lots of people have a bad start . . .

BROOKSIE No no, this is serious. My mother was eight days in labour with me.

ROSE Eight days?

BROOKSIE Yeah, eight days. She forgot to take her tights off.

ROSE What?

BROOKSIE I looked like a bank robber till I was six. Not easy walking about with a seam down the middle of your face. Thirteen of us little kiddies there were. Thirteen. And I was the youngest. All in the one room. And they all wet the bed. I could swim when I was two. I can still remember my mum putting me to bed saying, "Come on son, do you want the deep end or the shallow end?"

(*By now,* ROSE *cannot help herself, and is fighting not to laugh.*)

ROSE Idiot.

BROOKSIE It wasn't easy being that unlucky. In fact, if it weren't for bad luck I wouldn't have any luck at all. But I did get some good advice from my father. "Remember son," he said to me, "Always look out for number one, and be careful not to step in number two."

(*He moves round and sits on the sofa.*)

He was nice, my father. Do you know, he started walking five miles a day when he was sixty. Yeah. He's now eighty five and we don't know where the hell he is. What an upbringing. You can see where my confusion comes from, Rose. It makes me very nervous . . . especially with ladies. That's why I'm always overcompensating. And I was hopeless at chatting-up, too. Do you know what I said to a girl once? "Tell me, are you a model?" I said that. I really said that. Can you believe it?

ROSE And did she look like a model?

BROOKSIE Actually she looked like the back of a bus . . . but I was desperate at the time.

ROSE My favourite chat-up line was when this bloke said to me, "There's just something about you. I'm sure we must have met in a previous life."

BROOKSIE That didn't work on you?

ROSE Certainly not.

BROOKSIE Never worked when I used it either.

ROSE You didn't use that did you? (*He just laughs.*) Oh, you idiot.

BROOKSIE It's nice to see you laughing, Rose. You know, my mate Fred Minton used to say that to me when I was younger, "Make 'em laugh, that's the secret. Get them laughing, and you're half-way there." Trouble was, the only jokes I could remember weren't very funny.

ROSE Yes, I have to admit, your jokes are terrible.

BROOKSIE I know. (*He stops, and looks at her.*) Look, I'm sorry if I've upset you, Rose. I don't mean harm. It's just that . . . it's just that, I don't know the rules any more. I'm not one of your new-age men. I'm more of an old-age idiot. I just get so . . . so . . . lost at times. You know, since Grace . . . (*He stops, and pulls himself together.*) Sorry.

ROSE It's all right.

BROOKSIE So, Rose. I agree. I agree wholeheartedly to suspend hostilities. I want us to make peace, Rose. And I'd like us to try and keep the peace, if we can.

ROSE Yes, I'd like that, too.

(*He shifts across closer to her.*)

BROOKSIE And if the odd joke slips out now and again, don't get so grumpy with me.

ROSE That's difficult . . . but I'll try.

(*He again goes to shift closer to her. She points to the photo on the dresser.*)

Is that Grace?

(*He is caught mid-shift. He then rises and crosses to the desk.*)

BROOKSIE That's her. That's my Grace.

ROSE You loved her very much didn't you?

(*He brings the photo back to show her.*)

BROOKSIE I couldn't bear to be apart from her. Thirty-five years. I even hated going to work I missed her so much. And that was when she was alive. Now . . . it's very hard, Rose.

ROSE — I've been on my own for ten years now. He was much older than me, and a workaholic. Not what you'd call a scintillating marriage. It worked . . . but only just. Not a lot of laughter, that's for sure. So don't you get grumpy with me if I don't laugh at your jokes. I've not been used to it.

BROOKSIE — We must change that, Rose. You have a lovely smile. We should see it more often.

ROSE — Yes, well. (*She gets up.*) I'd better go. Thank you for this little chat. I feel better now.

(*He gets up, and places the photo on the sofa.*)

BROOKSIE — So do I, Rose. We should do it more often.

ROSE — Well, if you start getting silly again maybe we'll have to. Right. I'll, er . . . I'll see you tomorrow then.

(*She turns to leave.*)

BROOKSIE — Rose . . .

(*She stops.*)

Er . . . (*He moves to her, goes to say something, but then changes his mind.*) Er . . . see you tomorrow.

ROSE — Yes.

(*There is a moment between them. He then suddenly leans forward, and kisses her on the cheek. They are both startled.*)

BROOKSIE — Bye.

ROSE — Bye.

(*She hurriedly leaves.*)

BROOKSIE — See you tomorrow. (*He closes the door and comes back into the room. He raises his clenched fist in a gesture of triumph.*) Yes! Oh yes! (*He heads to the photo on the sofa.* GRACE *'appears' in the room through a hidden entrance between the front door and the main room alcove, and moves to behind him.*) Oh yes. I think I could quite easily suspend hostilities with Rose.

(*He picks up the photo of* GRACE *on the sofa.*)

BROOKSIE (*to photo*) Well? Was that OK?

GRACE That was OK. More like the Brooksie of old that was. You little charmer, you.

BROOKSIE (*to photo*) I was charming, wasn't I?

GRACE Still using the same old material I see, Brooksie.

BROOKSIE (*to photo*) Good to see the old material still works.

GRACE She's nice, Rose, isn't she?

BROOKSIE (*to photo*) Rose is nice, Grace. I like her very much.

GRACE She likes you, too.

BROOKSIE (*to photo*) I feel . . . different with her.

GRACE Perhaps you'll stop tickling the widows now.

BROOKSIE (*to photo*) Perhaps I should start behaving myself. But I do feel positive about her.

GRACE That's good. (*She looks at him a moment.*) You look a little smitten, Brooksie. Her plan is obviously working.

(*He stops, lowers the photo, and looks at her.*)

BROOKSIE Plan? You mean she's planning to get me?

GRACE Not in an obvious way. In her subconscious she's got it all planned, but in her conscious mind . . . well, she's still a bit torn at the moment. You've got a bit more work to do yet, Brooksie. But I think she's playing it very well.

BROOKSIE You make it sound as though I've got no choice in the matter.

GRACE You men never do have any choice in the matter.

BROOKSIE Oh, charming.

GRACE You never had any choice with me.

BROOKSIE Didn't I?

GRACE No. I chose you.

BROOKSIE Did you?

GRACE Yes. And now you're Rose's choice.

BROOKSIE Rose's choice?

GRACE And she'll be very good for you. Nice and feisty, but in a totally different way from me.

BROOKSIE Just take it easy with the matchmaking, Grace, it's early days yet.

(*He sits on the sofa.*)

GRACE No it's not. The time is right. And you have already kissed her.

BROOKSIE It was an innocent peck on the cheek, that's all.

GRACE It may have looked like that, but I know what you were thinking. And innocence is not something that comes naturally to you.

BROOKSIE Hey, that's not fair, Grace.

GRACE It may not be fair, but it's the truth.

(*He suddenly stops.*)

BROOKSIE Hold on a minute. How did you know I kissed her?

GRACE I told you before . . . I'm always with you.

BROOKSIE What, everywhere I go?

GRACE No, not everywhere. There are some places you're best left on your own.

BROOKSIE Thank goodness for that.

GRACE All you need to know at the moment, Brooksie, is that I approve of Rose. She's a bit of all right. (*She moves round behind him.*) Take me out of the equation, and move forward. (*She places her hands on his head.*) Life goes on Brooksie, life goes on. (*She lowers her hands, and starts to move away from him. He looks back at the photo.*) See you later. Try and get some rest, you've a long night ahead of you. (*She 'disappears' between the main room alcove and the stairs.*)

BROOKSIE Life goes on, eh Grace? Life goes on.

(*He remains looking at the photo. The lights snap off. End of Act One.*)

ACT TWO

The following morning.

SUE *is at the table busily buttering a pile of sliced bread. Also on the table are two other loaves of sliced bread, a large pot of tea, some milk, sugar, and several mugs.*

She looks at her watch, leaves the buttering, goes out into the hallway, and yells up the stairs.

SUE — Dad! Dad! Come on, the tea's ready. It's getting cold!

(*She comes back into the room, and heads for the table to continue buttering.* RICHARD *then enters through the front door. He is struggling with a large box containing bottles of wine, and two carrier bags containing cans of beer.*)

RICHARD — Hi. (*He sets the box and bags down.*) There we are. That should keep them all going for half an hour.

SUE — Do you want some tea? It's just made.

RICHARD — Quick one, then I'll go and get the buttonholes.

(*She starts to pour some tea.*)

SUE — Oh, thanks for doing all this, Richard.

RICHARD — That's all right. Is he up yet?

SUE — I've just called him.

RICHARD — Because it's no good him thinking he can lie in bed all morning. There's a lot to be done. It's not up to us to do everything. They're his friends.

SUE — He'll be down soon.

RICHARD Better be. Lazy little sod. And did you hear him come in last night?

SUE No. No, I didn't. Here's your tea.

(*She hands him the tea, and then continues the buttering.*)

RICHARD Thanks. Do you know what time it was?

SUE No idea.

RICHARD Four o'clock. Four o'clock he dragged himself in here last night.

SUE It was a stag night. You can't expect them to get back early. And please, I want no arguments today. It's Julia's wedding. It's a day of celebration, not recrimination.

(*He suddenly notices her buttering the bread.*)

RICHARD Excuse me, what are you doing?

SUE You can see what I'm doing.

RICHARD Well you can stop that right now.

SUE I'm just helping, don't fuss.

RICHARD It was his idea. He said he'd provide the sandwiches. Everybody's doing their bit for this reception, and that little sod's not getting out of it. We said we'd provide the buttonholes and some of the drink, he said he'd provide some sandwiches. He volunteered his services, not yours. Now please, stop what you're doing.

(*He goes to stop her. She slaps his hand.*)

SUE For goodness' sake, Richard, it's just a few slices of bread.

RICHARD I'm sorry, but he's not getting away with it.

(*He heads for the stairs.*)

SUE — Richard, I will not have arguments today, do you hear me?

(*He stops, and turns back to her. We then see* BROOKSIE *gingerly coming down the stairs.*)

RICHARD — It's his responsibility. He volunteered to do the sandwiches, and he's bloody well going to do them.

(BROOKSIE *appears in the alcove behind* RICHARD. *He looks rather the worse for wear.* RICHARD *turns, and yells.*)

Brooksie! Get down here now!

(BROOKSIE *almost rocks on his heels.*)

BROOKSIE — Oh my God! My head!

RICHARD — Good heavens. It's up and moving.

(BROOKSIE *staggers to the table.*)

SUE — There's some tea here, Dad.

(*She pours him some tea.* BROOKSIE *gingerly sits at the table.*)

RICHARD — That's it, you sit there. Now then, you see all that bread? That's for the sandwiches you're going to make.

BROOKSIE — Sandwiches?

RICHARD — You volunteered your services, now get on with it.

BROOKSIE — No thanks, I couldn't eat a thing.

RICHARD — They're not for eating, they're for making. Now get spreading.

BROOKSIE — Spreading?

Sue — Richard, leave him alone. Let him have some tea first.

Richard — (*leaning in to* Brooksie) You're not getting away with it, you know. I won't allow it. Everyone else is doing their bit, and you're going to do yours.

Sue — Here's your tea, Dad. (*To* Richard.) Let him have his tea.

Richard — He's not getting away with it, Sue.

Sue — Will you stop.

(Richard *looks at* Brooksie *for a moment.*)

Richard — Good night out last night, was it?

Brooksie — Yes, it was rather pleasant, thank you. Couple of drinks with the chaps, you know.

Richard — Really? Amazing how a couple of drinks can last till four in the morning. Dirty little stopout.

Sue — Richard!

Richard — So where did you go?

Brooksie — Er . . . (*He stops.*) Yeah, where did I go?

Richard — One of your dingy little dives, was it?

Sue — Richard, please, he's just got up.

Richard — Well, you'd better pull yourself together quick. There's a lot to be done here this morning.

Brooksie — Lot to be done? Can't you do it? I'm having my tea. (*To* Sue.) This is tea, isn't it?

Richard — Look at him, he's still drunk. When are you going to start acting your age?

Brooksie — I'll be all right as long as I don't start acting your age.

SUE Now that's enough, you two. I'm not having it today.

RICHARD I think I'll go and get the buttonholes. It's no good talking to him. It's like having a conversation with a chimpanzee. Except I'd probably get more sense from the chimp. (*He leans in close to* BROOKSIE.) I'm going to get the buttonholes now. I'm going to do my bit. When I get back, I want you to have done your bit. I don't want your daughter to have done it, I want you to have done it. Do you understand what I'm saying?

BROOKSIE Buttonholes?

RICHARD (*to* SUE) You're not to do it, Sue, do you hear me? I don't want you making those sandwiches. (*He suddenly stops.*) What am I saying? Why am I wasting my breath? Nobody takes any notice of me. Nobody listens. Why waste my breath? I'm only the bloke that lives here. I'm only the bloke that pays the mortgage. I'm only the bloke that pays the bills. So why waste my breath? (*He slowly starts heading for the front door.*) Why should anyone take any notice of me? I'm only the bloke that lives here. I'm only the bloke that pays the mortgage. I'm only the bloke that pays the bills. But why should that matter? Why should that make them listen? No reason at all. So why waste my breath? (*He is now at the front door.*) Why bother? I'm only the bloke that lives here. I'm only the bloke that pays the mortgage. I'm only the bloke that pays . . .

(*He has now gone. They sit staring after him.*)

BROOKSIE Er . . . I couldn't quite grasp what he was saying, Sue . . . what was all that business about sandwiches and buttonholes?

SUE He's right. You are still drunk. Why is it that men can't seem to enjoy themselves without getting drunk all the time?

BROOKSIE I don't know. Why is that?

SUE It's pathetic.

BROOKSIE It is pathetic.

SUE And there's such a lot to be done this morning, too.

BROOKSIE Everybody keeps saying that. What's got to be done? Give me a clue.

SUE I'll give you something in a minute. Really, Dad. Was Tom in the same state as you last night?

BROOKSIE Tom?

SUE That's all we need this afternoon. You two holding each other up. He could end up marrying the wrong woman.

BROOKSIE Tom. Marrying. Sounds like a hefty couple of clues there.

SUE And I hope you've got your speech sorted out. I don't suppose for one minute . . .

BROOKSIE Speech! Hold on, it's getting closer. Tom. Marrying. Speech. Yes, that's it! Tom's marrying Julia and I'm the best man. Sue, I'm the best man!

SUE God give me strength.

(*The front doorbell rings.* BROOKSIE *doesn't move.*)

SUE Please don't disturb yourself, I'll get it.

BROOKSIE Oh. OK.

(*She heads to the front door.* BROOKSIE *goes to get up.*)

Oh no, that's not wise. Shouldn't have done that.

(SUE *opens the front door.*)

SUE Oh, hello Rose, come in. Dad, it's Rose.

(ROSE *enters*, SUE *closes the door.*)

BROOKSIE Rose? Oh, hello Rose.

ROSE Brooksie.

BROOKSIE How nice to see you. Want some tea?

ROSE It's not a social call.

BROOKSIE What about bread? You want some bread? We've got plenty of bread here.

ROSE I think you know why I'm here.

BROOKSIE Don't tell me, let me guess. You were dreaming about me last night, and when you got to the cuddly bit . . .

ROSE I've had a phone-call from Julia.

BROOKSIE From Julia. That's nice.

ROSE It is not nice. She wants to know where Tom is.

BROOKSIE Tom?

ROSE He didn't go home last night, and she's very worried.

SUE Didn't go home?

BROOKSIE Didn't go home?

ROSE Oh, don't pretend you know nothing about it. (*To* SUE.) I told Julia I'd come round here and find out what's happened to him. I assume it's a sobering-up job. Probably too drunk to get home. God, these men. They're like children.

Sue — They're worse than children.

Rose — Drinking like that at their age. (*To* Brooksie.) Trying to be macho, were you? I suppose he's lying up there in a drunken stupor, is he?

Brooksie — Stupor?

Sue — I don't think he's here, Rose.

Rose — He's not here? (*To* Brooksie.) Isn't he here with you?

Brooksie — (*looking round*) He's not here.

Sue — Where is he then?

Brooksie — I don't know where he is. I'm not totally sure where I am yet.

Sue — What do you mean you don't know?

Rose — You must know what happened to him surely?

Brooksie — Well, something must have happened to him.

Sue — Dad, this is not funny. Julia is very worried.

Brooksie — Sue, I've told you . . .

Rose — Brooksie, if this another one of your silly jokes . . .

Brooksie — Jokes?

Sue — It's no good, we need to sober him up a bit. Look at the state of him. Dad, listen to me, and listen carefully. (*He fights to concentrate.*) We don't have time for all this . . .

Brooksie — Don't have time . . .

Sue — . . . there's a lot to be done this morning . . .

Brooksie — . . . lot to be done, yes . . .

SUE . . . we need answers . . .

BROOKSIE . . . answers . . .

SUE . . . and we need them now . . .

BROOKSIE . . . need them now, yes . . .

SUE . . . so if you're not sober enough to tell us where Tom is . . .

BROOKSIE . . . where Tom is . . .

SUE . . . then Rose and I will strip you off right here and now, and throw you into a cold shower.

BROOKSIE . . . cold shower, yes. Eh?

SUE That's right.

BROOKSIE Susan, this is your father you're talking to. You will do no such thing.

ROSE I will. You're not my father.

BROOKSIE Now, Rose, ordinarily I'd be very happy to get in a shower with you, but under the circumstances . . .

SUE Dad. What's happened to him?

BROOKSIE I've already told you, I don't . . .

SUE Right! Come on, Rose.

(*They grab him.*)

BROOKSIE No, hold it, hold it. Get off me! Rape! Rape! No wait, wait!

(*They stop, and release him.*)

SUE Now, start thinking clearly.

BROOKSIE Clearly . . . er . . . er . . . what was the question?

ROSE Right!

(*They go to grab him again.*)

BROOKSIE All right! All right!

(*They stop.*)

SUE Now, what's happened to him?

ROSE You must know what's happened. Didn't you come back together?

BROOKSIE Er . . .

SUE Well, did you or didn't you?

BROOKSIE Er . . . did we or didn't we . . . er . . . (*He suddenly stops.*) My God!

SUE What?

ROSE What?

BROOKSIE I can't remember. My God, I can't remember!

SUE Oh, I've had enough of this.

(*She grabs at him again.*)

BROOKSIE No, no! It's the truth. I swear.

(*She stops. He is clearly shocked by the realisation.*)

I can't remember.

ROSE He's covering something up.

BROOKSIE No . . .

SUE Are you covering something up?

BROOKSIE No, I'm not.

ROSE If you know something and you're not telling us . . .

BROOKSIE I don't know, I tell you! I really don't.

(*They both look at him for a moment.*)

ROSE — What do I say to Julia then?

BROOKSIE — I don't know.

(*The telephone rings.*)

SUE — I bet that's Julia. (*To* BROOKSIE.) You answer it.

BROOKSIE — Me? I can't answer it. What could I say?

SUE — What can I say?

BROOKSIE — I don't know.

SUE — (*looking at him*) The tonnage of information you don't know this morning must be some kind of record even for you.

(*She moves up to answer the phone.* ROSE *moves in to* BROOKSIE.)

ROSE — I thought things would be different after our talk yesterday, but I have to tell you, Brooksie, I am very, very disappointed with you.

BROOKSIE — Please, Rose, don't go on. My head's getting worse. And it was soft enough in the first place.

SUE — Rose, it is Julia. She'd like a word with you.

(ROSE *moves up and takes the phone.*)

ROSE — (*on phone*) Hello, Julia . . .

(SUE *moves down to* BROOKSIE.)

SUE — Dad, please . . .

BROOKSIE — Sue, how many more times . . .

SUE — Has he done a runner?

BROOKSIE — I wish I'd done a runner.

SUE — Come on, you can tell me. I know it can happen. People can get very nervous before a wedding. It's quite natural. It happened to me.

BROOKSIE — And you should have listened to yourself, instead of marrying that oaf.

SUE — Stop it. I won't have you talk about Richard like that. Anyway, we're not discussing us . . .

BROOKSIE — You brought it up.

SUE — . . . we're discussing Tom. Now, what did he say last night?

BROOKSIE — What did he say? I can't remember what he said. I can't even remember what he looks like.

SUE — Did he talk about running off? Did he seem nervous, anxious? What was his frame of mind?

BROOKSIE — It's my frame of mind I'm more worried about.

(ROSE *hangs up the phone, and moves down to them.*)

ROSE — He's still not back. She's in a terrible state. She's been phoning everywhere. (*To* BROOKSIE.) Surely you can remember something about last night.

SUE — Hold on a minute, hold on. Let's take this in sequence. Start at the beginning, and see if we can't jog something. (*She drags him to the sofa.*) Sit! (*He quickly sits.*) Dad, I want you to think carefully about last night. We're going to start at the beginning, OK?

BROOKSIE — OK.

SUE — Now you and Tom went out together for his stag night, is that right?

BROOKSIE — That's right. Stag night. Yes.

SUE Where did you go first?

BROOKSIE First. Where did we go first? Ah! We went somewhere first, I know that.

ROSE Oh this is just ridiculous. We don't have time for this. Julia said she's going to give it a little longer, and then she's coming round here.

BROOKSIE Coming round here?

ROSE She may have to contact the hospitals, and she wants to be with someone when she phones, just in case the news is bad. I mean, God knows what might have happened to him.

(*We hear* TOM *singing on the stairs. They all stop.*)

SUE Who's that?

ROSE Is that Tom?

(TOM *enters cheerily. He is not fully dressed.*)

TOM Morning all!

(SUE *and* ROSE *leap up.*)

SUE Tom! What are you doing here? I didn't know you were upstairs.

TOM Oh, sorry Sue. Didn't Brooksie tell you?

SUE No, he didn't tell me.

TOM He said I could crash out in the spare room last night.

ROSE Crash being the operative word, obviously.

TOM Well, it was a bit late.

SUE Yes, we know.

TOM And we were a bit the worse for wear.

Sue — Yes, we know.

Rose — Julia's been on the phone all morning. She's worried sick.

Tom — Is she? Oh dear. Why didn't you tell them, Brooksie?

Rose — It's no good talking to him. He doesn't know what planet he's on.

Tom — I'll phone her now. Can I have some tea first though Sue? Would you mind? I've got a throat like a baboon's armpit.

(Sue *goes to pour some tea.*)

Sue — Rose, would you like some?

Rose — I won't, thanks.

Tom — So, how are you then, Brooksie?

Brooksie — Earth.

Tom — What?

Brooksie — Earth. That's the planet. I know where I am now.

Tom — What a night, eh? Haven't seen you like that before. Never knew you could drink so much.

Brooksie — Did I drink?

Tom — Did you drink? Does a monkey have nuts? But I've been thinking about what you said, Brooksie, and I want you to know that I think you're right. And I want to thank you. It's not often people are that honest with each other.

Brooksie — (*he hasn't a clue*) Oh well, you know . . .

Tom — I know it will be difficult, but one has to be true to oneself, isn't that what you said?

BROOKSIE Er . . . yes . . . something like that.

TOM It's an important time in my life right now, and I've got to do the right thing. How best to break it to Julia, though?

SUE Break what to Julia?

TOM (*to* BROOKSIE) Haven't you told Sue yet?

BROOKSIE Er . . . told her what?

SUE (*giving* TOM *a mug of tea*) Told me what?

TOM Thanks. Well, Brooksie was giving me some good advice last night.

SUE Good advice? From him?

BROOKSIE Excuse me . . .

TOM He said some things that got me thinking, and I'm sorry . . . but I can't go through with the wedding. Right, Brooksie?

BROOKSIE Right. What?

ROSE } What?
SUE } What?

TOM I know it's come as a shock . . . but I'm not going to marry Julia.

(*They are all stunned.*)

ROSE I hope you're not serious, Tom.

TOM I'm deadly serious, Rose. It wouldn't be fair to her now. And with a friend like Brooksie to support me, as I know you'll support Julia, I'm sure we'll be able to see it through. Right, Brooksie?

BROOKSIE (*rising*) Er, Tom. I don't know what the hell I said, but I'm sure I didn't mean that you should call off the wedding.

Sue — Just a second. Let me get this straight. Are you saying that after taking advice on marriage from him, you have now decided to call off the wedding?

Tom — That's right.

Sue — I've never heard anything so absurd in my life. You said yourself how drunk he was. You can't possibly take seriously the ramblings of a drunken idiot like that . . .

Brooksie — Just a minute . . .

Sue — He has enough trouble communicating when he's sober.

Brooksie — I resent that!

Rose — How can you be so stupid, Tom? It's just the drink talking, can't you see that?

Tom — I take your point, Rose, but this was earlier in the evening, before he started falling over . . .

Brooksie — Falling over?

Rose — Falling over?

Tom — Don't worry, there were no broken bones. Although I was a bit worried when you crashed onto that table.

Brooksie — Crashed onto a table?

Rose — Crashed onto a table?

Tom — You see, sometimes a couple of drinks allows people to open up and say what they really feel, which they wouldn't do if they were sober. And I knew, as soon as I heard Brooksie saying it, I knew that it was true. I had this sort of, 'gut-feeling', you know?

BROOKSIE I'm starting to get a bit of a 'gut-feeling' now, too.

TOM And it made me feel really good.

BROOKSIE Well, it's making me feel a bit sick.

TOM Don't worry yourselves. If Julia is half the woman I think she is, she'll understand. As Brooksie said, there are things to do, places to go, people to see. Right, Brooksie?

BROOKSIE Er . . . listen, Tom . . .

TOM Everything's too comfortable. I've been seduced by comfort and security. Where's my danger? Where's the risk? Where's the excitement? Right, Brooksie?

BROOKSIE Tom. I'd be very much obliged if you'd stop saying "Right, Brooksie".

TOM Right, Brooksie. (*To* SUE.) Actually, Sue, I don't think I will phone Julia. I think this should be done face-to-face. This is eye-to-eye stuff, don't you think? (*He starts to head off.*) Will you all excuse me for a moment. I'll just go and sort myself out.

(*He then heads upstairs, singing. They are left, stunned.*)

SUE (*to* BROOKSIE) Well, what a night you had.

ROSE It seems you did a lot more talking than you did drinking. And you did a lot of drinking.

SUE (*moving angrily to* BROOKSIE) How could you do this to him?

BROOKSIE (*backing off round the sofa*) I don't remember doing anything to him.

SUE Why put all these ideas in his head?

BROOKSIE I didn't do anything.

SUE How could you?

BROOKSIE I didn't do anything.

(*He is forcibly stopped by* ROSE.)

ROSE And what's wrong with Julia, anyway?

BROOKSIE There's nothing wrong with Julia.

ROSE Why turn him against her then?

BROOKSIE I haven't turned him against her.

ROSE Of course you have. Why else would he call off the wedding?

BROOKSIE I don't want him to call off the wedding.

SUE Well, you certainly haven't been much help in that respect have you? Not exactly Cupid's little arrows you've been shooting round the room now, is it?

ROSE More like poisoned bloody darts if you ask me.

SUE Well, something's got to be done. And quick. You've got to talk to him and talk him out of it and talk him into his senses and talk him into not calling off the wedding, that's what you've got to do.

BROOKSIE Say that again.

SUE You know what I mean. Talk to him. Julia will be here shortly, and I want this wedding back on. Honestly . . . men.

ROSE Yes, men. You let them out for an evening on their own, and look what happens. They should have reins. Alongside the toddlers' reins in Mothercare they should bring in 'Men's Reins'. They'd make a fortune.

SUE Do you think we should ring Julia?

Rose I don't know. What do you think?

Sue I don't think we should tell her he wants to call the wedding off, but I think maybe we should just let her know he's all right.

Rose But he's not all right though, is he?

Sue (*indicates* Brooksie) Well, he'll have to make him all right.

Rose Perhaps it's pre-wedding nerves.

Sue Yes, I'd thought of that, too.

Rose Or the male menopause. Can he get a male menopause at his age?

Sue I don't know, it's possible I suppose. (*She looks at* Brooksie.) I mean, look at him. He's been in a state of menopausal idiocy for years.

Brooksie Excuse me . . .

Rose }
Sue } (*together*) Oh shut up!

(*We hear* Tom *returning down the stairs, singing.*)

Rose Here he comes.

Sue (*to* Brooksie) Talk to him.

Brooksie What can I say?

Sue I don't know. Things.

Brooksie What things?

Rose Any things.

(Tom *enters, now fully dressed.*)

Tom Right everybody. I'm off.

Brooksie Yeah, and I'm off, too.

(Brooksie *tries to go.* Rose *grabs him.* Sue *rushes over to* Tom.)

Sue — Hold on, Tom.

Tom — Thanks for the hospitality, Sue, and I'm sorry you've gone to . . .

Rose — Please, Tom. Before you see Julia, we need to talk to you.

Tom — Rose, it's no good you saying anything . . .

Sue — Wait, Tom, wait. Brooksie needs to talk to you.

Brooksie — Do I?

Sue — (*very firmly*) Yes!

Rose — (*whacking him*) Yes!

Tom — (*moving down to them*) Listen, girls, don't look so worried. It's all right. Julia will understand. Besides, it wouldn't be fair to marry her now. I'm going to change. I'm going to be different. I can't marry her, and then change my whole life. I must change it first, sort it out, and then marry her. If she'll still have me of course. She might not like me when I'm different.

Rose — But you could lose her, don't you see that?

Tom — I do, Rose, but as Brooksie said, in every man's life, at some point, there has to be sacrifice. He said that.

Brooksie — Do me a favour, Tom. Don't keep telling me what I said. Understand this. I don't usually drink very much. Therefore, when I have two pints I am almost drunk. That is like someone else having six or eight pints. Now if someone who has had six or eight pints told you that you shouldn't get married, you would have serious reservations about his judgement, because you'd think his head had gone soft. Well, I'm sorry to have to admit this to you, but when I told you those things, my head had gone soft too. In fact, it's been soft since. And it's getting softer by the minute.

TOM You're just trying to protect me, I realise that.

BROOKSIE I'm not! I'm trying to protect myself.

(*He sits on the sofa.* TOM *moves and sits in the armchair.*)

TOM But I haven't had the courage to change until now. That's what you gave me last night. The courage to at least try. If things don't work out, so what? That's not failure. Not trying is failure. That's what you said, Brooksie. You said that.

ROSE (*sits on sofa*) What is all this nonsense about changes, Tom? Why do you need to change?

TOM There's all kinds of things I haven't done, Rose. I'm not saying I regret my life, it's just that I haven't done enough. And if I don't do it now, I'll never do it. I'll be old soon.

BROOKSIE You're old now, you idiot.

TOM But as you said Brooksie, "You're only young twice". And this opportunity mustn't be wasted, My eyes have been opened.

ROSE And your brain has closed up.

SUE But I don't understand . . . what is it that you want to do, Tom?

(TOM *rises and moves behind the sofa to* SUE.)

TOM I don't know, all kinds of things. For example, I've never been hang-gliding before.

ROSE Hang-gliding?

TOM — Or bungee-jumping. Although I'm not too sure about that. I've never flown on Concorde. I've never ice-skated. All these things are possible. There's a whole load of countries I've never seen. I've never been to a Test Match in Australia. I'm not saying I'll do any of these things, but I want the possibility to be there. I want to be able to dream. And who knows what might happen? I could end up dancing across the mountains on the moon.

(SUE *and* ROSE *turn and look at* BROOKSIE.)

BROOKSIE — Mountains on the moon? I never said that, surely.

ROSE — (*rising, to* TOM) Julia was going to phone the hospital to see if you were all right. I think she should phone and have you admitted.

TOM — All right, all right, maybe I'll never get to the moon, but you get my point.

SUE — We know what you're saying, Tom, but it's the kind of thing everyone says when they're out drinking.

TOM — You know the happiest time of my life? When I was in the RAF. I had wonderful times. I'm not saying I didn't enjoy my job after I left, I did, but I've never reached my full potential. I'm capable of more. When I was in the RAF, I felt I could have done anything. I want to feel like that again.

ROSE — We all want to feel like that, Tom, but life moves on. Even if the brain wants you to do something, the body doesn't always allow it.

TOM — But we mustn't be restricted by physical limitations. That's what Brooksie said. (*To* BROOKSIE.) Remember? "You're only young twice". And you're right. I've been a miserable, complaining little sod. But you've lifted me. And now . . . (*He sits on the sofa beside* BROOKSIE.) I want to be like him.

ROSE What?

SUE Like him?

TOM A free spirit. He does things I wouldn't dream of doing. He rides a motor-bike, something he's always wanted to do. He stays out late, he's noisy, he's untidy, and he doesn't care what people think of him. And people like him for it. They think he's funny.

SUE Not everybody likes him, I assure you.

ROSE And not everybody thinks he's funny, either.

TOM Well, I think you're funny, Brooksie.

BROOKSIE Yeah, but you're an idiot, so where does that leave me?

TOM Watching you do these things, Brooksie, makes me want to do them too. I'd love to be banned from the Over-60s club.

BROOKSIE I'm not banned.

TOM Well, you certainly wouldn't be very welcome, not after what you did to Gladys Porter.

BROOKSIE (*quickly rising*) It wasn't me.

ROSE What did he do to Gladys Porter?

BROOKSIE They couldn't prove I did that.

SUE What did he do?

TOM (*rising*) I know they couldn't prove it. But we all knew it was you. No one else would have done it.

ROSE — What did he do?

TOM — You see, that's the point, Rose. If something happens, no one tries to accuse me. They know I wouldn't have done it. Well it's not good enough . . . I want a reputation!

BROOKSIE — You can have mine. I'm fed up with it.

TOM — And I'm going to have a reputation. You'll see once we get our flat together.

ROSE — Flat?

SUE — What flat?

TOM — Didn't Brooksie tell you? We're getting a flat. That's the plan, isn't it Brooksie?

BROOKSIE — (*sinking into the armchair*) Flat?

SUE — (*to* BROOKSIE) And how long have you been planning this?

TOM — Nothing too expensive, mind. I need to be able to afford the hang-gliding lessons. Independence, that's what we want, eh Brooksie? Go to bed when we want, get up when we want, do the washing-up when we want. As Brooksie said, no more of these petty household restrictions.

SUE — (*glaring at* BROOKSIE) Petty household restrictions, I see.

(BROOKSIE *sinks even further into the chair.*)

TOM — Not too far from the pub, either. We want to be able to walk home. No driving, in case we've had a few too many sherberts. Music, dancing, late-night parties . . . independence. Right, Brooksie?

SUE — I can't stay here listening to this. Come on, Rose, let's go into the other room. Leave them to it. (*She grabs* BROOKSIE *by the collar.*) You.

Talk to him. I want this wedding back on. I don't care what you have to do, just get it back on. And before Julia gets here, too.

(SUE *and* ROSE *head for the room off the hallway.*)

TOM Julia's coming round here? Oh, right, I'll have another cup of tea, then.

(ROSE *exits into the room.* SUE *stops at the door, and turns back to* BROOKSIE.)

SUE And if it's not back on by the time Julia gets here, you'll be the one going off to the moon. I'll kick you there myself!

(*She turns, and slams the door behind her.*)

TOM Oh dear. Bit upset, aren't they? Still, I suppose it's understandable. Shall I get the tea, or will you?

BROOKSIE Tom . . .

TOM I'll get it then.

(*He crosses to the table to pour some tea.*)

BROOKSIE Tom, listen to me . . .

TOM It's no good, Brooksie, my mind is made up.

BROOKSIE (*rising*) You have a lovely lady and a lovely life. You can't just throw it all down the pan.

TOM But it's not the life I want, Brooksie.

BROOKSIE (*crosses to* TOM) You've been happy with it up to now.

TOM Ah, but have I?

BROOKSIE What about Julia? You still love her don't you?

TOM Of course I do, but as you said, "You're only young twice".

BROOKSIE Yeah, well I'm going to be dead twice if you don't change your mind. Julia will kill me first, and then Rose'll leap in just to make sure.

TOM I'm not going to change my mind. This is a new start for me.

BROOKSIE Start for you, and the end for me.

TOM It's not your fault, Brooksie. You just got me thinking, that's all. Sugar?

BROOKSIE Forget the tea. I need something stronger.

(*He moves up and takes a can of beer from one of the carrier bags.*)

TOM Oh, I didn't see all that there. I think I'll have one of those as well.

(BROOKSIE *gets one for* TOM *and brings it to the table.*)

No, don't blame yourself, Brooksie, you've done me a real favour.

BROOKSIE Listen, you idiot, I was drunk. Do you understand? I was drunk. I didn't mean any of it.

TOM It doesn't matter that you didn't mean it. It set the ball rolling.

(BROOKSIE *opens the can. It squirts all over the table. They mop it up with slices of bread.* BROOKSIE *then moves across and sits on the sofa.*)

BROOKSIE Oh for God's sake, see sense, Tom. It was just drunken nonsense.

TOM Brooksie, enough. Please accept my decision. There's nothing you can do about it. I'm not going to change my mind.

BROOKSIE Oh, Tom . . .

(TOM *moves across and sits on the sofa.*)

TOM My life's been too sheltered. Out of the RAF, and straight into a marriage. Don't get me wrong. It was a wonderful marriage, and my Mary was a wonderful wife. When she went, I was out of a marriage and into my daughters. Then I was out of my daughters and into Julia's. It's been too sheltered. I'm out of touch with the real world. The world's changing, and I'm not. I've got to keep up.

BROOKSIE It's best not to keep up sometimes. These changes in the world aren't always for the better, you know.

TOM I know. But I feel like an alien sometimes.

BROOKSIE We all do. Everybody over thirty feels like an alien these days. I don't know, all these changes. Do you know what happened to me the other day? I was out on the motor-bike, and some bloke cut me up really badly. Swerved right in front of me. I nearly had an accident trying to avoid him. I beeped my hooter at him, and he just stuck his finger up at me, like this.

(*He sticks up his middle finger.*)

BROOKSIE No apology. No acknowledgement of the fact that it was his mistake. Oh no. Just this. (*He sticks up his middle finger again.*) And what is that anyway? Not only was I insulted, I didn't even know what the insult meant. I mean, what happened to the two-fingers? We all know what the two-fingers mean. "I don't think you're a very nice person". "I don't think you've got a very pleasant disposition". We all knew where we stood with the two-fingers. So why did they get rid of them? And when did they get rid of them? I didn't know. No one told me. And who got rid of them? Who decided? It's all nonsense. Well I want the two-fingers back. All these stupid changes. That's the trouble with the world today, too many changes.

Tom — Careful, Brooksie, you're sounding like me. Or rather, you're sounding like the old me. This country's changing. I've got to adapt and start enjoying myself.

Brooksie — Problem is, that all the people who really know how to run this country are busy driving taxis and cutting hair. And you won't change. You'll read an article in the paper about teenage vandalism, and the old you will come charging back all guns blazing.

Tom — It won't happen, Brooksie, you'll see. I'm determined to enjoy myself And the first thing I'm going to do is get back into the dancing.

Brooksie — Dancing?

Tom — Dancing, yes. I love my dancing. Always have done. That's how I used to get the girls. Oh yes, I had style in those days. The pasa doble and the tango were my specialities.

Brooksie — You used to dance the pasa doble?

Tom — I went in for competitions. Oh yes, I could glide you across a floor like you've never been glided before.

Brooksie — Really? Well I'll give that little avenue of excitement a miss if you don't mind.

Tom — I've got medals you know.

Brooksie — Oooh. And did you dress up?

TOM Dress up?

BROOKSIE You know, sequins and things.

TOM Actually, there weren't so many sequins around in my day. Lot of taffeta, I seem to remember.

BROOKSIE I bet you looked lovely.

TOM Not me you dope, the ladies.

BROOKSIE What did you wear then?

TOM Never you mind.

BROOKSIE No come on. What did you wear?

TOM You wouldn't believe me if I told you.

BROOKSIE Try me.

TOM All right then. (*He rises.*) If you must know, I used to grace the floor in a glittering, midnight blue, skin-tight cat-suit.

BROOKSIE A midnight blue skin-tight . . . I'd have paid money to see that. I was never what you'd call a dancer . . . although I was told once I had a very funny twist.

TOM I can believe it. The twist. What a common little gyration that was. That's not dancing. I always refused to do it, did something else instead. Did you know you can fit the tango to the twist? Oh yes.

(*He suddenly bursts into song, and sings the first verse of 'Let's Twist Again' while dancing the tango to the rhythm of the twist.* BROOKSIE, *enjoying the moment, leaps up and starts to twist energetically as he sings the middle section of the song. They sing the last verse together as* BROOKSIE *twists and* TOM *tangos. They end together with a flourish.* BROOKSIE *twists his back.*)

BROOKSIE Oh my God, my back!

(TOM *holds him up.*)

TOM That's the trouble with you old twisters . . . no suppleness. Doesn't matter if you lose your teeth and lose your hair . . . staying supple, that's the key.

BROOKSIE Staying supple? I'm having trouble staying upright.

(TOM *helps him across, and they both now sit back on the sofa.* BROOKSIE *looks at him a moment.*)

Oh, Tom, what am I going to do with you? Listen, seriously . . .

TOM Please, Brooksie, no more. Please. My mind is made up.

BROOKSIE So that's it then, is it?

TOM That's it. (*He looks at the piles of bread on the table.*) I'll pay back what's been spent. Don't want anyone out of pocket. Do you think we should start clearing this lot up? You know, as a sort of gesture. (*He gets up and crosses to the table.*) I know it's not going to stop them being angry, but it's something isn't it?

BROOKSIE (*rises and follows him*) Listen. If I'm going to die soon, and I'm sure they're out there planning a very grisly death for me even as we speak, I would like to end my days doing something slightly more enjoyable than clearing up bits of bread.

TOM Friend of mine had a great way of getting rid of unwanted bread. We'd be in a restaurant somewhere . . . and he used to roll it into a little ball . . . (*He demonstrates by rolling up some bread into a ball.*) . . . and then discreetly fling it over his shoulder. Carried on with his meal, no one knew what was happening. Like this.

(*He flings the bread ball over his shoulder.*)

BROOKSIE Hey, don't do that. (*He goes to pick it up.*) I thought we were supposed to be clearing up, not making more mess.

(*He finds the bread ball, and goes to put it in the wastepaper bin.* TOM *meanwhile has made another one, and as* BROOKSIE *bends over to get the bin*, TOM *throws it at him.*)

BROOKSIE Hey!

(TOM *throws another one as* BROOKSIE *gets the bin.*)

TOM Hold out the bin, Brooksie.

BROOKSIE Eh?

(TOM *flicks another breadball into the air.*)

BROOKSIE Careful, careful!

(*He catches it in the bin.*)

TOM Bravo! Now put it on your head . . . I like a bit of a challenge.

(BROOKSIE *holds the bin on his head, and* TOM *flicks another one, basketball fashion, at the bin.* TOM *tries this a few times.*)

BROOKSIE Hang on, you're having all the fun.

(*He then positions the bin on the sofa, and hurries across to the table.*)

TOM Frisbee, Brooksie . . . frisbee.

(*They then empty the two loaves of bread onto the table, and start trying to frisbee the bread into the bin, laughing as they abandon themselves to the childishnes . . . then* TOM *hits* BROOKSIE *in the face with one of the slices. They then start throwing the slices at each other.* BROOKSIE *rushes out and uses some of the bread strewn all over the floor to get back at* TOM. *He throws 'hand-grenade' fashion, through his legs, etc, until finally he charges in using the bin for protection.*)

BROOKSIE I'm coming in!

TOM I surrender! I surrender!

(*They end up round the table, exhausted, and howling with laughter.* SUE *and* ROSE *come bursting in.*)

SUE What the hell is going on in here?

(*They both guiltily, and quickly, stop.* SUE *and* ROSE *survey the bread-strewn scene.*)

SUE Dear God.

BROOKSIE We were just trying to help clear up a bit.

SUE This is clearing up, is it?

ROSE I've seen tidier two-year olds.

SUE And take that bread off your head.

(BROOKSIE *sheepishly removes the slice of bread plastered to the top of his head.*)

So. Do I assume from the level of enjoyment that the wedding is back on?

BROOKSIE Er . . .

TOM No, Sue, the wedding is not back on. This was part of the celebrations.

SUE What celebrations?

TOM The birth of the new me. The start of my new life.

ROSE Tom. You have got to pull yourself together. Julia will be here any minute.

TOM Rose, please, what do you want me to do? Make her unhappy?

ROSE You are going to make her unhappy.

TOM Not in the long run.

SUE (*to* BROOKSIE) Some help you've been.

BROOKSIE I tried. I tried.

(*He picks up his can of beer. She snatches it away from him.*)

SUE Give me that! Honestly. We're worried to death out there, and you're in here behaving like two drunken yobbos.

TOM I told you, Sue, it's a celebration.

SUE I don't want to know! If Julia wasn't coming round I'd kick you both into the street. Well, go and get your little flat. Good riddance to the pair of you.

ROSE Brooksie, please, you have got to make him see sense.

BROOKSIE There's nothing I can do, Rose. His mind is made up.

TOM My mind is made up.

BROOKSIE He's not going to change it.

TOM I'm not going to change it.

BROOKSIE It doesn't matter what I say.

TOM It doesn't matter what he says.

BROOKSIE Will you shut up?

TOM Will you shut up? Oh, sorry.

(*The front doorbell rings.*)

SUE There she is! Tom, please.

TOM I'll talk to her. Stop worrying, she'll understand.

ROSE I'll go.

(ROSE *heads for the door.*)

TOM Don't say anything to her, Rose. I want this to come from me. Well, this is it, Brooksie. Wish me luck.

BROOKSIE Forget the luck, just make sure you tell her it's not my fault.

SUE And I'll make sure I tell her it is your fault.

(ROSE *opens the door.*)

ROSE Hello, Julia. Come in.

(JULIA *enters, and crosses towards* TOM.)

JULIA Hello, Tom. Found you at last.

TOM Yes.

JULIA At least you're safe.

SUE (*under her breath*) Only just.

TOM Julia, I'd like to talk to you. (*He turns to* SUE.) Sue, could we go in the other room, please?

SUE Of course.

JULIA I think it's better to talk in here, Tom.

TOM No, this needs to be in private.

JULIA I mean, it's better for me to be in here, Tom. I have something to say, and I think I'd like the others here when I say it.

TOM Julia . . .

JULIA No, Tom. I need to speak first. And please, try not to interrupt me. I'm sorry . . . but I can't go through with the wedding.

(*They all stop, stunned.*)

TOM What did you say?

JULIA Last night, when we were out on our hen night, Rose said some things that got me thinking . . . and I'm sorry, Tom, I know this is going to hurt you . . . but I don't think we should get married at the moment.

TOM Julia.

BROOKSIE Rose said some things?

ROSE Julia, I don't understand. I didn't say anything to . . .

JULIA It's all right, Rose. I know you weren't aware of the impact your words had on me, but you made me see sense. And I want to thank you. You were a true friend to me last night.
It's not often people are that honest with each other. It was wonderful advice, and I see things clearer now.

ROSE But Julia . . .

JULIA I know you didn't realise you were giving advice . . . we were just talking . . . but it made me think. You opened my eyes Rose, and gave me the strength to go through with this.

BROOKSIE Rose said some things?

JULIA (*turning to* SUE) I'm sorry, Sue, all the trouble you've gone to.

SUE (*shocked*) It's all right, Julia.

JULIA I'll make sure you're not out of pocket. (*She turns to* TOM.) And now maybe we should go into the other room and talk about it. (*To* SUE.) Is that all right, Sue?

SUE Of course.

JULIA (*to* TOM) Unless you don't want to talk to me now.

TOM No no, of course I do.

JULIA Well, as long as you're sure.

(*They head for the upstage room.* JULIA *then stops and turns back to* ROSE.)

And thanks again, Rose. You're a real friend.

(*They exit into the room. The others are left, still stunned.* BROOKSIE *finally breaks the silence.*)

BROOKSIE Rose. How could you?

ROSE Oh shut up.

SUE What did you say to her?

ROSE I don't remember saying anything to her.

BROOKSIE Well you must have said something, Rose. (*He is relishing this.*) How could you? I mean, what have you got against Tom? Don't you want Julia to many him?

SUE Stop it, Dad, don't be so mean.

BROOKSIE Mean? You were very quick to pick on me the pair of you. Well . . . I just don't know what to say, Rose. How could you?

ROSE I told you to shut up.

SUE God, what a day. Right. I'd better go and find Richard. Get him to take the buttonholes back.

ROSE Sue . . . I'm sorry. I . . . I don't know what to say . . .

SUE Don't worry about it, Rose, it's all right. My father told me that life is full of surprises. He didn't tell me he'd be the cause of most of them.

ROSE Oh, Sue . . . and all this trouble you and Richard have gone to. All this food and drink.

BROOKSIE I'd suggest a party, but I'm not sure I want to be seen in public with you, Rose, not after this. Going round breaking up people's marriages.

SUE Stop it, Dad. If Richard comes back tell him I'm out looking for him.

(*She leaves.* BROOKSIE *just looks at* ROSE. *She is still clearly shocked.*)

BROOKSIE Oh Rose, Rose, Rose.

(ROSE *moves down and sits on the sofa.*)

ROSE I just can't imagine what I could have said.

BROOKSIE I'm sure I don't know either, Rose.

ROSE I did have a couple of glasses of wine. That wouldn't have helped.

BROOKSIE Doesn't sound much.

ROSE It is for me. I'm not really a drinker.

BROOKSIE Like me then.

ROSE No, not like you, thank you very much.

BROOKSIE I think we could do with a drink now though, Rose.

(*He goes to the drinks cabinet.*)

ROSE I just can't remember what we were talking about. Oh, I feel terrible.

BROOKSIE You and me in the same boat, Rose. Ah well, let's look on the bright side. We might have done them a favour.

ROSE But they seem so right for each other,

BROOKSIE Ah, but who can tell, Rose. (*He brings down the drinks and sits on the sofa.*) You see it all the time. Couples that seem like a union made in heaven end up getting divorced in six months, while the couple that people don't give a cat-in-hell's chance to, survive against all the odds. You just can't tell.

(*He gives her the drink.*)

BROOKSIE I mean . . . look at you and me. When I first saw you, I thought, now there's a nice-looking little dish, I wouldn't mind getting to know her better. Then I started to get to know you, and I thought . . . hold on a minute . . . she's a bit too grouchy for me, this one. But then . . .

ROSE What do you mean grouchy? I'm not grouchy.

BROOKSIE Hang on, I haven't finished.

ROSE How can you say I'm grouchy? You can call me all sorts of things, but not grouchy.

BROOKSIE Just let me finish, will you?

ROSE When was I grouchy then? Come on, tell me when I was grouchy.

BROOKSIE Rose, I'm trying to make a point here.

ROSE Well, I don't want to hear it, thank you.

BROOKSIE Will you let me finish. What I was about to say was . . .

ROSE You're no angel yourself, you know?

BROOKSIE No, that's not it. Anyway, we're not talking about me.

ROSE In fact, if we're talking about who's grouchy around here . . .

BROOKSIE Will you be quiet and listen to me!

ROSE Don't you talk to me like that!

BROOKSIE (*forcefully*) I was trying to say, I then got to know you better, realised you weren't grouchy, and that in fact you were the kind of woman I'd be very happy to spend the rest of my life with! That's what I was trying to say!

ROSE You think I'd spend my life with someone as grouchy as you?

BROOKSIE Well then, it doesn't matter what I thought, does it?

ROSE No!

(*They turn away from each other and take a drink.* ROSE *suddenly stops.*)

You'd be happy to spend the rest of your life with me?

BROOKSIE I'm not so sure now.

ROSE But that's . . . that's . . .

BROOKSIE Look, just forget I said anything. I shouldn't have said anything.

ROSE But that's such a . . . nice thing to say to someone.

Brooksie — Well, don't sound so shocked. I'm quite capable of saying something nice now and again.

(*There is a moment.*)

Rose — Well . . . I don't quite know what to say.

(*He looks at her.*)

Brooksie — Listen, Rose. What do you think?

Rose — Think about what?

Brooksie — You and me?

Rose — You and me? What about you and me?

Brooksie — Come on, Rose, you know what I'm talking about.

Rose — I'm not sure that I do.

(*He moves in closer to her.*)

Brooksie — I'd like us to go out on a date.

Rose — A date?

Brooksie — Yes, a date. You know what a date is. Your memory can't be that bad.

Rose — (*she looks at him*) I don't know that I'm ready for this, Brooksie. I don't know that I'm ready for you.

Brooksie — I don't know that I'm ready either. But I think it's worth a try, Rose. No harm in trying, is there?

Rose — No. I suppose there's no harm in trying.

Brooksie — Great. Pick you up at seven-thirty?

Rose — Tonight? Isn't that a bit soon?

BROOKSIE No, tonight's fine. We were going out anyway.

ROSE Yes, to their wedding!

BROOKSIE Yeah. We've managed to stop that happening between us. But you've bought a new outfit, Rose. Be a shame not to show it off.

ROSE (*she looks at him*) It's a very expensive outfit. Would have to be somewhere nice.

BROOKSIE Are you crazy? Of course it'll be somewhere nice. You're going out with Gordon 'Brooksie' Brooks. No fish and chip shop for you and me. Great, that's settled then. One thing though, Rose. If we're going out together, promise me something.

ROSE What?

BROOKSIE No getting grouchy, OK?

(*She playfully slaps his leg. He then quickly puts his hand on top of hers. She looks at it a moment, then quickly pulls her hand out from underneath, and puts it on top of his. They do this a few times, giggling, then stop and look at each other. He then leans in to give her a kiss on the lips. She tilts her head back.*)

ROSE Now now. I don't do that sort of thing on a first date.

BROOKSIE You don't?

ROSE No.

BROOKSIE Oh well, forget it then.

ROSE What?

BROOKSIE (*laughing*) I'm joking. I'm joking.

ROSE You know, I'm not sure this is such a good idea.

(*Just then*, JULIA *enters*.)

JULIA — Sorry to interrupt.

ROSE — Julia.

JULIA — Would you mind coming in for a moment, Rose?

ROSE — (*hurriedly getting up*) No, of course not. Is everything all right?

JULIA — Yes, it's fine. Excuse us, Brooksie. (*To* ROSE.) Just need a bit of advice.

ROSE — I see.

(*They turn to leave*.)

BROOKSIE — Need any advice from me, Julia?

(*She turns back to him*.)

JULIA — I've just been hearing about your advice.

BROOKSIE — Oh. Right.

(*They leave*.)

BROOKSIE — A date. She's agreed to a date. (*He clenches his fists in a gesture of triumph*.) Yes! Oh yes!

(*He then looks across, and moves over to the desk*. GRACE *'appears' from the entrance between the main room alcove and the stairs, and moves across to him*.)

I've got a date, Grace.

GRACE — Good for you.

(*He picks up the photo*.)

BROOKSIE — (*to photo*) Mind you, she was in a slight state of shock at the time. I think I might have caught her unawares.

GRACE You caught us all unawares, Brooksie.

BROOKSIE (*to photo*) Hope she doesn't realise and change her mind.

GRACE She won't change her mind. She'll have doubts . . . as any sensible woman would . . . but she'll turn up.

BROOKSIE (*to photo*) Forgive me, Grace.

GRACE There's nothing to forgive. I told you, the time is right. It's meant to be, Brooksie, and the process has started. It's important that you and Rose get together. You have a journey to make, and lessons to learn from each other.

(*He lowers the photo and looks at her.*)

BROOKSIE Steady on, Grace. All this talk of journeys and lessons. We're only going on a date.

GRACE And remember, Brooksie, it is a first date. Play it gentle. No behaving like you did with me.

BROOKSIE What do you mean? I was the soul of chivalry on our first date.

GRACE Until we were left on our own, and then your hands were everywhere.

BROOKSIE I didn't notice you putting up too much of a struggle, though.

GRACE Never mind that. Rose is different from me. Don't rush it.

BROOKSIE At my age I need to rush it. I haven't got that much time left.

GRACE There's time, Brooksie, there's time.

(*She moves closer to him.*)

And Brooksie . . .

(He turns to her.)

We won't be talking like this again.

(He looks at her for a moment, and then slowly nods.)

It'll be a different kind of communication. I'll always be with you, one way or another . . . but it'll be . . . different.

BROOKSIE (*quietly*) Will I know it's you?

GRACE (*she nods*) You'll know it's me.

(She then reaches out, and places her hands on his head. He closes his eyes.)

Do your best, Brooksie. Just do your best.

(There is a moment. She then takes her hands away.)

See you, Brooksie.

(He still has his eyes closed.)

BROOKSIE See you, Grace.

(She starts to move away. He opens his eyes.)

BROOKSIE Hold on a minute.

(She stops.)

That first date of ours. I seem to remember it was you that started all that.

GRACE What?

BROOKSIE It was your hand that made the first move. My hands only got going once I'd got the lead from you.

GRACE That is absolutely not true.

BROOKSIE Yes, it is. I remember it quite clearly now. Your hand went right down . . .

GRACE No, it didn't, And even if it did, it was a defensive gesture.

BROOKSIE Defensive? Down there?

GRACE I was fending off a full-frontal attack.

BROOKSIE You were being saucy, Grace. Come on, admit it. No need for coyness now.

GRACE Coyness? I don't think I've ever been called coy before. (*She laughs, and moves in close to him.*) I don't think it matters how it started. I'm just happy that it did start.

BROOKSIE So am I, Grace. So am I.

(*They look at each other for a moment. The moment is then broken as* ROSE, JULIA, *and* TOM *return.* BROOKSIE *is slightly thrown to see them.*)

Oh. Hi.

TOM Don't look so worried, Brooksie. It's all right, we're fine. No bones broken.

ROSE Do you mind if I get us all a drink, Brooksie? I think we could do with one.

BROOKSIE No, no of course not. I'll, er . . .

ROSE It's all right, I'll do it.

(ROSE *goes to the drinks cabinet.*)

BROOKSIE (*fighting to concentrate on them*) So. Everything's all right then is it?

JULIA Everything's fine, Brooksie.

TOM A truly momentous day, wouldn't you say? The start of my new life.

JULIA And mine.

(GRACE *moves to between* TOM *and* JULIA, *turns back to* BROOKSIE, *and blows him a kiss*.)

BROOKSIE Yeah. The start of mine, too.

ROSE Right. Drinks!

(GRACE *moves up as* ROSE *replaces her between* TOM *and* JULIA. *She gives them the drinks*.)

ROSE (*to* JULIA) There we are, Julia. That should keep your nylons up. Isn't that what you say, Brooksie?

(ROSE *heads back to the drinks cabinet.* TOM *moves across to beside* JULIA. GRACE *is now by the exit between the main room alcove and the stairs. She waves at* BROOKSIE. BROOKSIE *discreetly waves at* GRACE. ROSE *moves down and puts the drink into the hand* BROOKSIE *was waving*.)

ROSE There you go, Brooksie. Get that down your screech.

(GRACE *waves again, and then leaves*.)

BROOKSIE (*fighting to concentrate on* ROSE) Eh?

ROSE Get that down your screech.

BROOKSIE Screech? You're a bit chirpy, Rose.

ROSE No point in being any other way. Right. A toast. To Julia and Tom.

BROOKSIE Julia and Tom.

ROSE And may they have a very long and a very happy marriage.

BROOKSIE A very long and a very happy . . . (*He stops.*) Marriage?

TOM It's back on, Brooksie!

BROOKSIE What?

ROSE Oh yes!

JULIA A proper toast!

ROSE A proper toast! One, two, three, four . . .

(*They go into their previous toasting routine.*)

"Here's to the wedding of Tom and Julia,
Some might think that the union is peculiar,
We don't . . ."

BROOKSIE Hold it! Hold it!

(*He eventually manages to stop them.*)

BROOKSIE What happened? What the hell happened?

(JULIA, TOM, *and* ROSE, *then all start talking animatedly together.*)

TOM (*together*) It's amazing, Brooksie. Once we got talking we realised we were both worried about our independence . . .

JULIA We never really talked it through, you see, and I was very worried . . .

ROSE They were frightened of hurting each other's feelings and both felt they were being selfish . . .

(*They continue ad-libbing loudly and animatedly in this vein, until* BROOKSIE *eventually manages to stop them.*)

BROOKSIE Hold it! Hold it! Some sense please! Some sense!

Tom (*excitedly*) The point is, Brooksie, we realise we both want the same things . . .

Julia . . . and we both want our independence . . .

Tom . . . and we both want to be different . . .

Julia . . . and we both want to do new things . . .

Tom . . . and we both don't want to be bogged down by safety and security . . .

Julia . . . and we both want to go hang-gliding . . .

Tom . . . so if we both want to do all those things, why shouldn't we do them together?

Julia And it wouldn't have happened without you two.

Tom You've forced us to talk to each other.

Julia Thank you. Both of you. You're real friends.

Tom Yeah, thanks. (*He stops.*) There's one thing worrying me though, Brooksie.

Brooksie What's that?

Tom I'm really sorry about the flat.

Brooksie (*he laughs*) Don't worry about it, Tom. I'll survive.

Tom And there's another thing that worries me, too. (*He looks at* Julia.) She's very interested in that bungee-jumping idea.

Julia Can we do it off the Eiffel Tower?

Tom The Eiffel Tower?

Rose A toast!

BROOKSIE A proper toast! One, two, three, four . . .

(*Again they go into their toasting routine.*)

"Here's to the wedding of Tom and Julia,
Some might think that the union is peculiar . . ."

(RICHARD *and* SUE *enter. They are obviously shocked at what they see, and try to stop the commotion.*)

RICHARD } What the hell's happening now?
SUE } What's going on?

(BROOKSIE *stops the toast, and crosses to them.*)

BROOKSIE Sue, the wedding's back on!

SUE Back on?

BROOKSIE Richard. Go back and get them buttonholes!

RICHARD Buttonholes?

(BROOKSIE *goes back to the others.*)

BROOKSIE Come on, gang.

RICHARD Terrorists!

BROOKSIE One, two, three, four . . .

(*The toast continues loudly. The lights fade.*)

The end.

FURNITURE AND PROPERTY LIST

Further furniture and dressing to be added at the director's discretion.

ACT ONE

Scene One

On stage: Sofa.
Armchair.
Drinks cabinet. *On it:* a selection of bottles and glasses, a telephone.
Desk. *On it:* table-lamp, framed photograph of GRACE, various papers, pens, etc.
Dining-table. *On it:* tablecloth, 2 or 3 items of crockery.
4 dining-room chairs.
Bay-window curtains.

Off stage: Crash-helmet, scarf, gauntlets (BROOKSIE).

Scene Two

Strike: Crash-helmet, scarf, gauntlets, tablecloth, used glasses.

Set: On dining-table: *Trivial Pursuit* game, 4 coffee mugs.

On drinks cabinet: fresh glasses.

Off stage: Drying-up cloth (TOM).

ACT TWO

Strike: *Trivial Pursuit* game.

Set: On dining-table: small dish containing butter, knife, 2 plates, some buttered bread and some to be buttered, 2 further loaves of sliced bread (opened), tea-pot, milk-jug, sugar bowl, 6 mugs, 2 drying-up cloths.

Off stage: Wine-carrier with 6 bottles of wine, carrier bag full of cans of beer (RICHARD).

LIGHTING PLOT

Property fittings required: Table-lamp.

ACT ONE

Scene One

Late evening.

To open: Full lighting including practical table-lamp.

Cue 1:	As RICHARD enters from kitchen RICHARD switches off kitchen light. (Page 2)
Cue 2:	BROOKSIE: . . . we all have to be miserable?" BROOKSIE switches off main room lighting, leaving hallway light on and the table-lamp on. (Page 23)
Cue 3:	BROOKSIE: "I've forgotten who the real me is." BROOKSIE switches off the table-lamp. (Page 27)
Cue 4:	BROOKSIE exits up the stairs. After a moment hallway light snaps off. (Page 27)

Scene Two

Afternoon.

To open: Full lighting.

No cues.

ACT TWO

Morning.

To open: Full lighting.

No cues.

EFFECTS PLOT

ACT ONE

Scene One

Cue 1: RICHARD: I'd rather it was sooner."
Motorbike arrives. (Page 4)

Cue 2: SUE: . . . other people live in this house too."
Car arrives, horn beeps loudly. (Page 8)

Scene Two

No cues.

ACT TWO

Cue 3: SUE: "God give me strength."
Front doorbell rings. (Page 55)

Cue 4: BROOKSIE: "I don't know."
Telephone rings. (Page 59)

Cue 5: TOM: "Will you shut up? Oh, sorry."
Front doorbell rings. (Page 84)

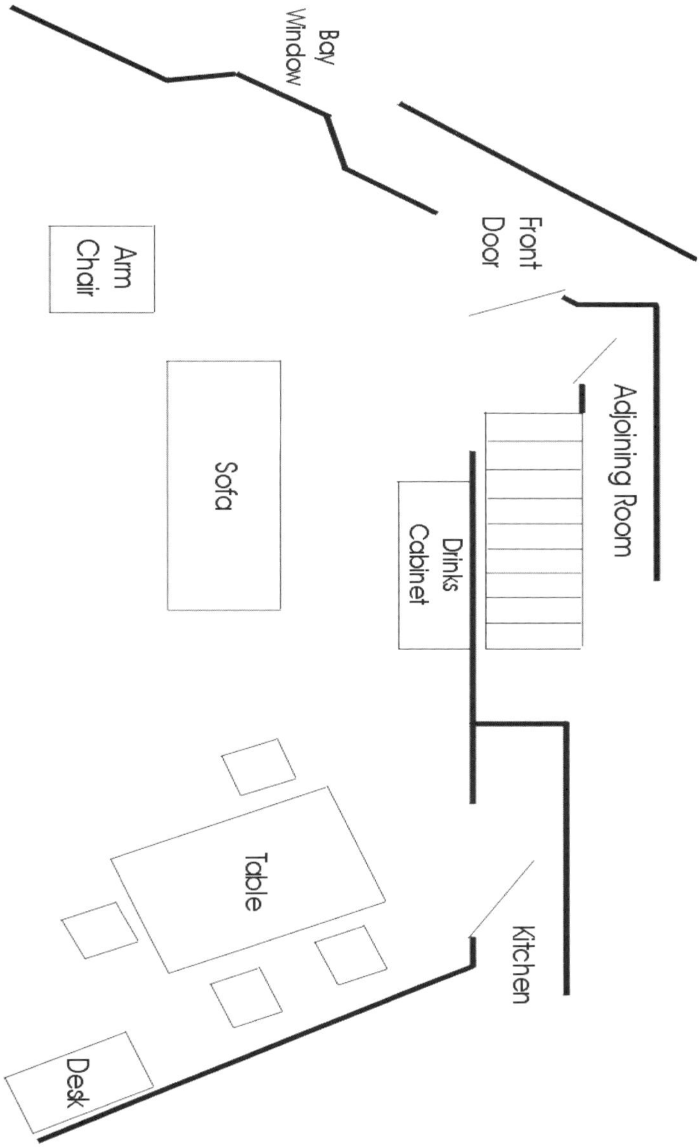
Bay Window
Front Door
Arm Chair
Sofa
Adjoining Room
Drinks Cabinet
Table
Kitchen
Desk